# 世界旧石器技术
# 虚拟仿真实验教程

## World Paleolithic Technology Virtual Simultation Experiment:
## A Practical Coursebook

## （中英双语）

主　编　李英华

副主编　周玉端

参　编　娄文台　王　凤　杨濡僖

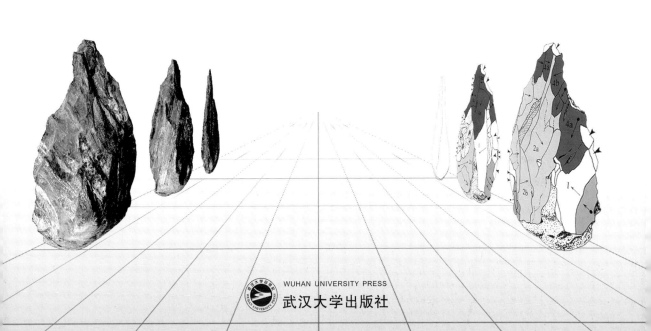

WUHAN UNIVERSITY PRESS

武汉大学出版社

**图书在版编目(CIP)数据**

世界旧石器技术虚拟仿真实验教程:汉、英/李英华主编.—武汉:武汉
大学出版社,2024.8
ISBN 978-7-307-24416-0

Ⅰ.世… Ⅱ.李… Ⅲ.旧石器时代考古—计算机仿真—实验—高等学
校—教材—汉、英 Ⅳ.K86-39

中国国家版本馆 CIP 数据核字(2024)第 109346 号

责任编辑:李晶晶 责任校对:鄢春梅 版式设计:马 佳

出版发行:**武汉大学出版社** (430072 武昌 珞珈山)
(电子邮箱:cbs22@whu.edu.cn 网址:www.wdp.com.cn)
印刷:武汉中科兴业印务有限公司
开本:787×1092 1/16 印张:15.5 字数:317 千字 插页:1
版次:2024 年 8 月第 1 版 2024 年 8 月第 1 次印刷
ISBN 978-7-307-24416-0 定价:59.00 元

# 总 目 录

世界旧石器技术
虚拟仿真实验教程

# 前　言

　　最近十多年虚拟仿真实验课程和各类慕课迅速发展，知识的传授不再局限于某个学校的课堂，这也使得建立一门全国性的关于旧石器技术学的课程成为可能。由于旧石器技术研究需要频繁使用世界各地的石器标本，需要对石器标本进行精确的三维展示和观察，而虚拟仿真技术恰好可以成为这门课程的有力助手。于是，基于虚拟仿真技术的"世界旧石器技术虚拟仿真实验课程（中英双语）"软件应运而生。

　　从20世纪60年代起，"操作链"理念下的技术研究逐渐成为旧石器研究的主流方法与目标。这个源自法国的旧石器研究潮流，在经历近30年的发展后，形成了具有特色的技术学理论与方法体系。20世纪90年代，随着中外学术交流的开放和增多，法国的旧石器研究理论和方法传入中国旧石器考古学术界，为中国学者带来了新的研究思路，并推动了中国旧石器研究的国际化。最近20年，受到法国学者的直接影响，技术研究逐渐成为中国旧石器研究者的主要研究方法，并在实践中不断运用，在产生大量成果的同时也带来了关于它的疑惑和实践上的误差，其中一个重要的原因是研究者对其缺少系统的学习和全面的理解，国内尚无一个具有普适性的关于旧石器技术学的课程，学习者大多通过个人理解和老师们的经验传授来学习这门课程。这种情况也导致对于相关概念的理解因人而异，不同研究者难以在同一个层面上进行学术交流。面对这种情况，亟待开设一门系统的旧石器技术学的课程，而且这门课程要能够尽可能多地让国内学生接触到，甚至是参与到课堂中来。

本教程主要包括知识学习和考核学习两个核心部分。其中，知识学习主要介绍旧石器技术学的相关概念和术语、基本的打制概念和产品、打制工艺、石器拼合实验、石器技术阅读和石器技术绘图等。考核学习主要是通过回答问题的形式，一方面考察知识学习的成效，另一方面加深巩固前面所学内容。另外，教程还提供了相关的文献资料，汇总了旧石器技术学研究的核心文献，方便学生课后查阅和深入学习。本虚拟仿真实验课程是本科生课程"远古人类文化与技术""考古与人类文明进程""世界旧石器考古"和研究生课程"旧石器时代考古""石器鉴定与研究"的一部分。在教程编写方面我们依次介绍了各个模块的操作，学习者在具体使用过程中不必拘泥于此顺序。

旧石器技术学是一种需要将理论与实践相结合并不断练习运用的研究分支，也是一个需要在不同研究者之间开放交流、相互探讨的领域，更是需要在"透物见人"的最终解释层面深度思考、谨慎考量的体系，只有这样，才能真正触及石器技术的逻辑和规律，做到"透石见人"。希望本虚拟仿真课程能够为建立相对统一的旧石器技术研究体系贡献一份力量，更重要的是激发读者在今后的石器研究中主动运用技术学的思维。

本教程对应的"世界旧石器技术虚拟仿真实验课程（中英双语）"软件开发得到了武汉大学长江文明考古研究院、实验设备处的资助，所用三维模型的石器标本除自有收集以外，主要得到了法国巴黎第十大学 Eric Boëda 教授、法国人类古生物研究所 Henry de Lumley 教授的允准和法国自然历史博物馆 Stéphanie Bonilauri 副研究员的协调支持，还得到了湖北省文物考古研究院、云南省文物考古研究所、广西文物保护与考古研究所、湖南省文物考古研究院、重庆中国三峡博物馆等单位的大力支持。石器三维模型的构建除了本教程署名的团队研究生外，法国自然历史博物馆的博士研究生黄孙滨、硕士研究生 Marie-Josée Angue Zogo 给予了重要帮助。三维建模软件由武汉大势智慧科技有限公司提供。中科院古脊椎动物与古人类研究所、北京大学、吉林大学、山东大学、浙江大学、河北师范大学、中央民族大学、湖北大学、中南民族大学、山西大学以及武汉大学历史学院和法学院等单位的前辈和同行在三维建模、教学实践和课程申报方面或与本书主编进行过有益的探讨和交流，或提供了专业指导，或给予了关心和支持。考古系多位教师在实验软件维护、项目实施、软著申请等方面给予了帮助。学校组织的数次评审中专家们提出了很多建设性意见，推动了软件和课程的不断改进和提高。此处未能一一列举，谨致谢忱。

最后，由于作者水平和时间有限，虚拟仿真实验软件和教程中难免存在纰漏与错误之处，还请读者朋友不吝指正。

作者

2024 年 2 月 1 日

# 目 录

# 绪　论

石器是古人生产、生活中常用的工具，通常带刃，具备切割、砍砸、刮削、挖钻等功能。旧石器时代晚期至新石器时代的石器形态、结构相对规整（如镞、斧、锛、凿等），比较容易辨识和类比，而旧石器时代早中期的石器形态极不规整，因而仅仅根据形态难以深入揭示打制者的生产概念与方法、工具的性质及其内在逻辑。本实验将以旧石器技术研究理论为指导，以考古遗址出土的石制品为研究对象，以动态、整合的方式重建石器从原料选择到毛坯制作再到刃口形成的"操作链"，从而揭示和理解打制者的意图与认知，探索世界范围旧石器技术与远古人类文化的共性与差异性。

## ◎ 实验步骤：

登录武汉大学虚拟仿真实验教学项目管理平台查找本项目（https：//xfsy. whu. edu. cn/website/resources/list. action），或打开网址（http：//210. 42. 121. 113/ShiQi/）进入"世界旧石器技术虚拟仿真实验"网站首页，点击"实验原理"按钮，进入"实验原理"部分（图 0-1）。理解石器的重要性以及石器技术研究对于我们复原石器的打制过程、解释打制者的意图、探索石器技术演化和远古人类文化多样性的重要意义。

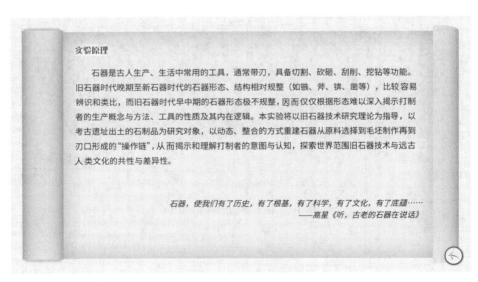

图 0-1　实验原理界面

# 第1章 探索之旅

◎ 实验步骤：

回到"世界旧石器技术虚拟仿真实验"网站首页，点击"探索之旅"按钮，出现一张世界地图(图1-1)，依次(或随意)点击非洲、欧洲、亚洲、美洲、大洋洲地图的范围，网页界面弹出各大陆旧石器文化概述的窗口，阅读理解该大陆的旧石器文化概况。

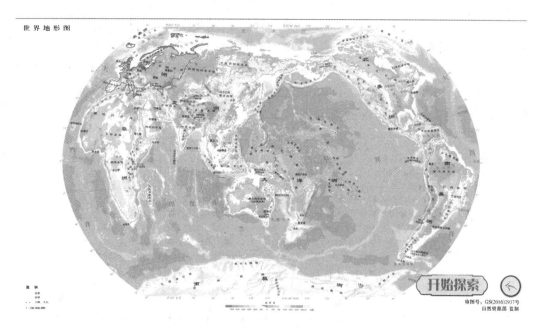

图1-1 探索界面的世界地图

# 1.1 世界旧石器文化概述

## 1.1.1 非洲旧石器文化概述

非洲的旧石器时代从330万年前开始,直到9000年前左右才开始逐渐进入新石器时代,但各个地区并不同步。非洲大陆具有最漫长的旧石器时代,旧石器时代的每个阶段几乎都早于世界其他地区。非洲旧石器技术与文化的多样性远远超出克拉克线性的"模式 I-V"的归纳。非洲旧石器文化的发展序列采用了不同于欧洲的术语:石器时代早期(Earlier Stone Age)、石器时代中期(Middle Stone Age)和石器时代晚期(Later Stone Age)。这些术语本身既反映了特定的学术史背景,也与该区域旧石器技术的地方性特征密不可分。非洲旧石器时空分布范围很广,技术内涵十分丰富(图1-2)。

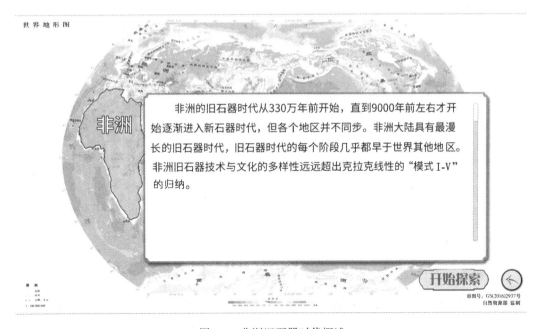

图 1-2 非洲旧石器时代概述

## 1.1.2 欧洲旧石器文化概述

最早的欧洲人出现在150万—120万年前,欧洲旧石器时代一直延续到距今1.1万年前后,其旧石器技术具有一定程度的地区差异。西欧和南欧的旧石器文化发展序列比较清晰,石器技术文化的演化经历了不同的阶段:前阿舍利时期(Pre-Acheulian)—阿舍

利 时 期 （ Acheulian ）—莫 斯 特 时 期 （ Mousterian ）—沙 特 佩 罗 尼 亚 文 化 时 期
（Châtelperronian）—奥瑞纳文化时期（Aurignacian）—格拉维特文化时期（Gravettian）—梭
鲁特文化时期（Solutrean）—玛格德琳文化时期（Magdalenian）。中欧、东欧与西南欧相比
有较大的地区性差异，无法用西南欧的技术历史来概括它们旧石器文化的阶段特征。欧
洲旧石器时空分布范围广，技术内涵也十分丰富（图 1-3）。

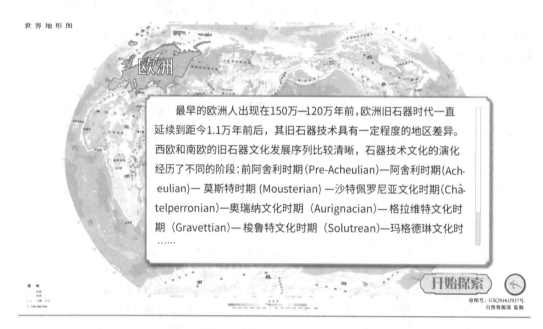

图 1-3　欧洲旧石器时代概述

## 1.1.3　亚洲旧石器文化概述

亚洲旧石器时代至少从 250 多万年前开始，一直延续到 1 万年前左右。亚洲旧石器
技术具有明显的地区多样性，除南亚、西亚外，中亚、北亚、东亚和东南亚整体上经历
了一条不同于地中海及其周边地区（西欧与非洲）的石器技术演化道路，只有少数区域
或遗址因文化交流或技术的重新发明而出现与地中海世界相似的技术产品。东亚地区的
石器技术演化以连续继承为主，同时可见东西方文化交流或本土创新，在距今 5 万—4
万年出现明显的技术变革，进入旧石器时代晚期。亚洲旧石器整体上时空分布范围广，
技术内涵十分丰富（图 1-4）。

图1-4 亚洲旧石器时代概述

## 1.1.4 美洲旧石器文化概述

美洲的旧石器时代至少始于4万年前，相当一部分遗址距今2万—1.5万年，直到距今1万年左右进入古代期或古印第安时期(美洲的旧石器时代晚期)，其旧石器时代结束的时间在美洲大陆年代跨度较大，从距今7000年到3000年左右，而且空间分布不平衡。传统上认为美洲人最早的文化是克洛维斯文化(Clovis Culture，始于1.35万年前)，但是最近20多年的考古发现和研究越来越多地揭示出前克洛维斯文化(Pre-Clovis Culture)的存在。前克洛维斯文化并不是一个统一的文化实体，而是由年代为距今大约1.4万年的一系列遗址构成，这些遗址展示出与克洛维斯文化截然不同的技术和工业类型。目前，北美洲最早的考古遗址的年代距今约13万年前(有较多争议)，而中美洲和南美洲已经发现了100多个年代范围为距今1万—5万多年的遗址地层，这些遗址可以充分说明美洲人类石器技术发端的时间比以往认识的要早得多，而且其演化路径和内涵与旧大陆有显著区别(图1-5)。

世界地形图

美洲的旧石器时代至少始于 4 万年前，相当一部分遗址距今 2 万—1.5 万年，直到距今 1 万年左右进入古代期或古印第安时期（美洲的旧石器时代晚期），其旧石器时代结束的时间在美洲大陆年代跨度较大，从距今 7000 年到 3000 年左右，而且空间分布不平衡。传统上认为美洲人最早的文化是克洛维斯文化(Clovis Culture, 始于 1.35 万年前)，但是最近 20 多年的考古发现和研究越来越多地揭示出前克洛维斯文化(Pre-Clovis Culture) 的存在。前克洛维斯文化并不是一

......

开始探索

审图号：GS(2016)2937号
自然资源部 监制

图 1-5 美洲旧石器时代概述

## 1.1.5 大洋洲旧石器文化概述

大洋洲最早有人类居住的时间可以追溯到 6.5 万年前，如澳大利亚北部卡卡杜国家公园发现的 Madjedbebe 岩厦遗址表明人类 6.5 万年前可能跨过了宽达 80 ~100 公里的海面到达此地生活。该遗址的石器组合包括磨石、磨碎的赭石、磨刃的斧头、一些打制的石片工具、可能被用作矛头的尖状器以及加工食物的工具。其中，磨制石器是世界上最早的，年代为 5 万年前。遗址中有很多赭石块和相关的加工工具。距今 5 万年之后，大洋洲地区遗址的数量增多，不局限于澳大利亚，周围岛屿如新几内亚东部 8 个高地遗址的发现证实在 4.9 万—4.4 万年前，人类已经在这里制作和使用石器用来开发动植物资源，发现的打制石器包括以砾石为原料的石核、石片、石斧等。1 万—0.8 万年前，新几内亚东部高地出现了仅刃部和器身磨制的斧-锛类器物，以东的岛屿还发现了距今约 0.8 万年的石片石器工业。而最早居住在美拉尼西亚以东、以北大片岛屿的人类是南岛语族，其技术与文化演化路径不同。由于岛屿和海洋环境的差异，大洋洲整体石器技术具有地区多样性，难以与旧大陆的旧石器时代进行对比，部分打制石器在这些地区遗址的使用直到欧洲殖民者的到达为止(图 1-6)。

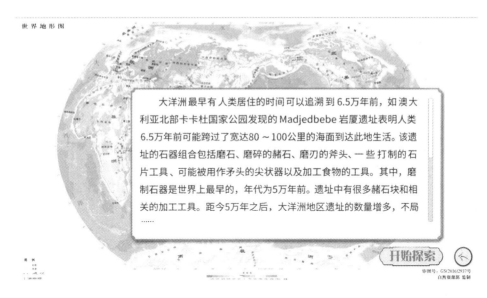

图 1-6 大洋洲旧石器时代概述

## 1.2 石器认知学习

◎ **实验步骤:**

进入"开始探索"后,点击"石器认知学习"模块,学习基本的石器知识(图 1-7)。

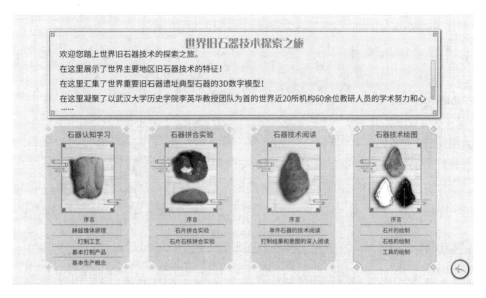

图 1-7 世界旧石器探索之旅

### 1.2.1 序言

石器认知学习是旧石器技术研究的基础部分。在该模块，学生需要理解并掌握赫兹锥体原理、打制工艺、基本的打制产品和基本的生产概念等内容（图1-8）。

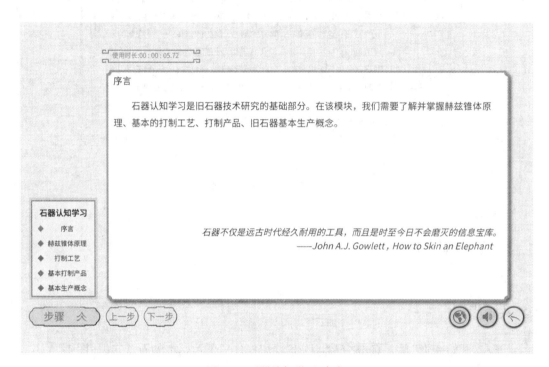

图1-8　石器认知学习-序言

### 1.2.2 赫兹锥体原理

◎ **实验原理：**

赫兹锥体是物体穿过固体时产生的锥体，如子弹穿过玻璃。严格地说，它是一种从撞击点穿过具有脆性、非晶态或隐晶态固体材料时形成的力的锥体。这个力最终在原料上留下一个完整或不完整的锥体。这种物理原理可以解释石制品制作过程中片疤的形态和特征（图1-9）。

◎ **实验步骤：**

点击"下一步"，进入赫兹锥体原理的学习，之后有一道选择题供学生学以致用，完成后会显示正确答案和解析，学生可根据答案判断自己是否掌握知识点。

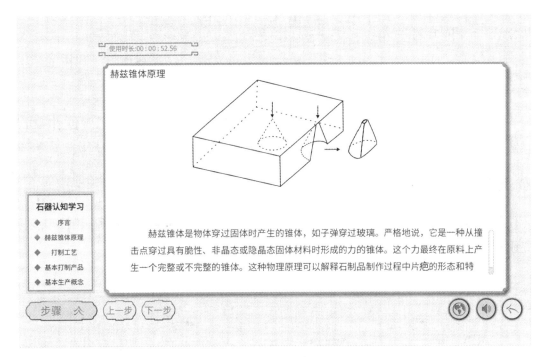

图 1-9　赫兹锥体原理图示与解释

点击"下一步"，出现一道学以致用的选择题（图 1-10）。

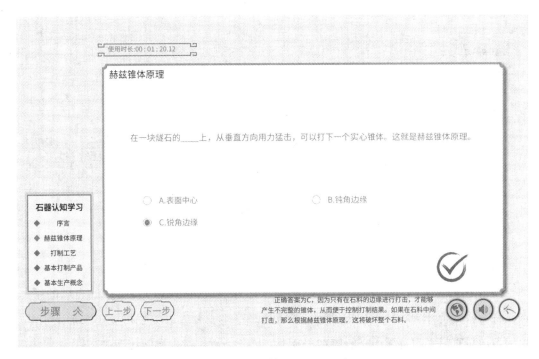

图 1-10　赫兹锥体原理的学以致用

## 1.2.3　打制工艺

### ◎ 实验原理：

工艺一般是指剥离下石片所采用的施力、打制手段以及动作姿势，通常包括锤击、碰砧、砸击、摔碰和压制等工艺。工艺属于打制石器技术系统知识的初级层次。

### ◎ 实验步骤：

点击"下一步"，进入打制工艺的学习，依次学习锤击、碰砧、砸击和压制等工艺，完成学以致用的选择题，巩固知识，加深印象(图1-11)。

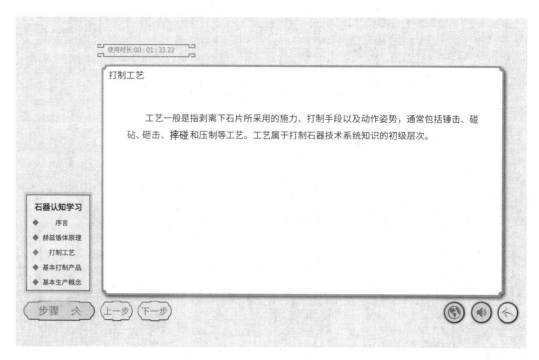

图 1-11　打制工艺的解释

(1)锤击法。

锤击是运用石锤，集中力量，借助赫兹锥体原理，打击石料表面靠近边缘的某一点，将石料剥裂开的一种工艺与过程，既可用来产生石片毛坯，也可以用来加工工具。根据石锤与原料之间有无中介的存在，锤击又可分为直接锤击和间接锤击(图1-12)。

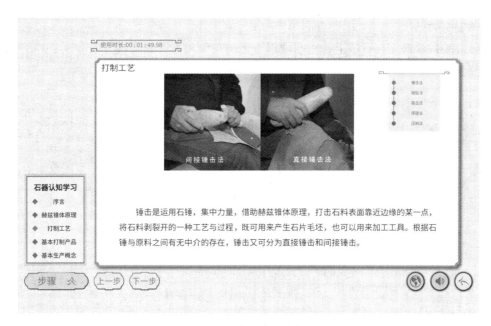

图 1-12　锤击法图示与解释

（2）碰砧法。

碰砧是用手持石料，向另一石块，即石砧上碰击以便剥裂石片的工艺与过程（图 1-13）。

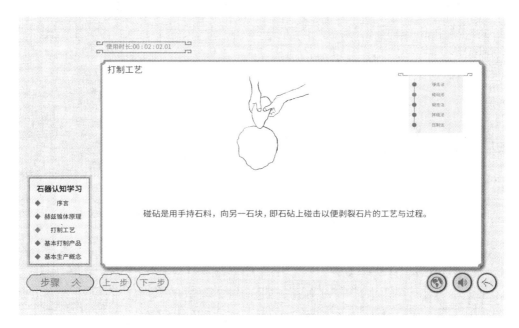

图 1-13　碰砧法图示与解释

（3）砸击法。

砸击是将石料垫在石砧上，用石锤以合适的角度和力度砸石料，以分裂石料的工艺与过程(图 1-14)。

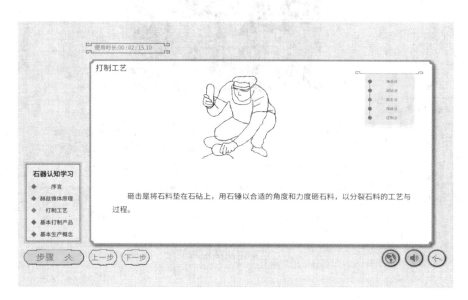

图 1-14　砸击法图示与解释

（4）摔碰法。

摔碰是采用站立的姿势，将手中的石料摔投到石砧上，从而使原料碎裂的一种工艺(图 1-15)。

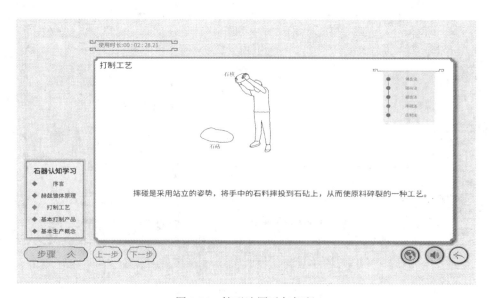

图 1-15　摔碰法图示与解释

(5)压制法。

压制是用一个很尖的工具压石块或石片、石叶的边缘使之更加规整的工艺，可以用来加工工具，也可以剥离细石叶(图 1-16)。

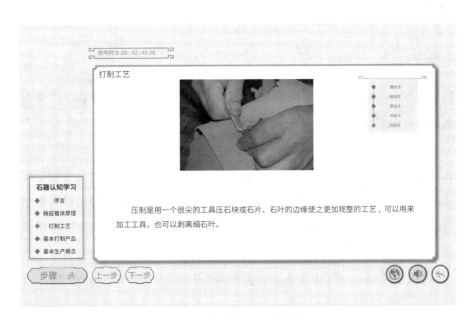

图 1-16 压制法图示与解释

点击"下一步"，进入一道学以致用的选择题(图 1-17)。

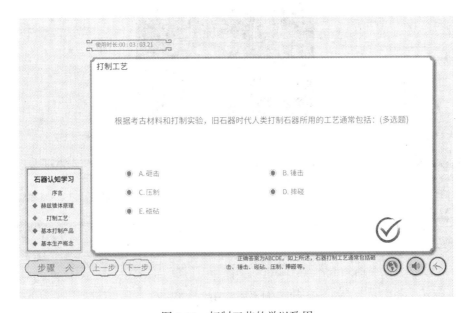

图 1-17 打制工艺的学以致用

## 1.2.4 基本的打制产品

### 📋 原料的认识

#### ◎ 实验步骤:

依次点击"下一步",进入原料学习的环节,结合石器图片及石器三维模型了解三种不同的原料:砾石、灰岩角砾以及矿脉结核。

(1)砾石。

砾石是远古人类在河滩拣选的用于打制石器的原料,通常是经过流水搬运冲磨和风化后形成的表面光滑、无尖锐棱角的天然岩石,也称为河卵石。因搬运距离和水流动能不同,河卵石表面磨圆度有差异。河滩上的砾石通常都被搬运,远离其原生矿脉,属于次生埋藏。地质学上根据尺寸又将其分为细砾、粗砾和巨砾。旧石器考古中一般以 7 厘米为界(也有以 10 厘米为界)将砾石分为大型砾石(Cobble)和小型砾石(Pebble),超过 25 厘米者为巨型砾石(Boulder)(图 1-18)。

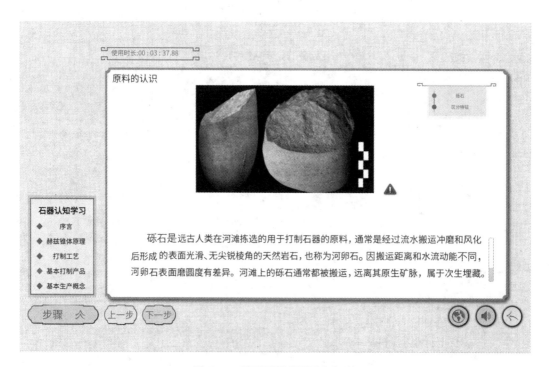

图 1-18 砾石原料的图示与解释

点击"下一步"，可见对砾石区分特征的解释（图1-19）。

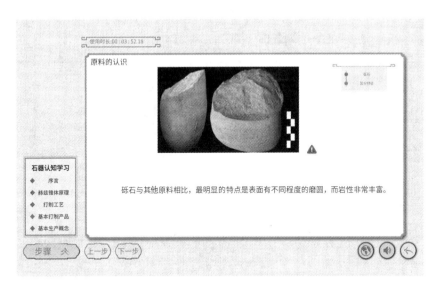

图1-19　砾石的区分特征

（2）灰岩角砾。

石灰岩洞穴或岩厦中因风化等原因剥落下来的块状岩石称为灰岩角砾，其主要矿物成分为碳酸盐、碳酸钙，硬度较燧石等略低，因风化或水作用程度不同表面棱角尖锐程度有差异，有些表面还有钙质结核附着。远古人类常从灰岩角砾中拣选合适的石块用作打制石器的原料（图1-20）。

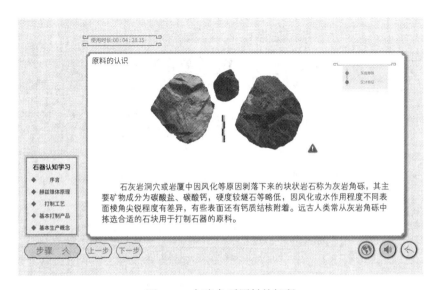

图1-20　灰岩角砾原料的解释

点击"下一步",可见对灰岩角砾区分特征的解释(图1-21)。

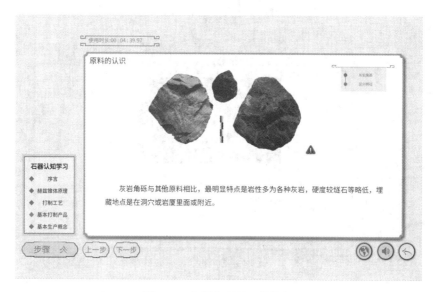

图1-21 灰岩角砾的区分特征

(3)矿脉结核。

矿脉结核是远古人类在山区岩矿条带堆积处开采的用于打制石器的原料,地质学上是指在成分、结构、颜色等方面与围岩有显著区别,且与围岩间有明显界面的矿物集合体。它们往往发育在山脉岩层中,古人开采的通常是这些矿物集合体里面经风化或其他原因暴露、剥落下来的质地相对均匀、各向同性的岩块或结核,其未经过水或风力等的搬运,属于原生埋藏(图1-22)。

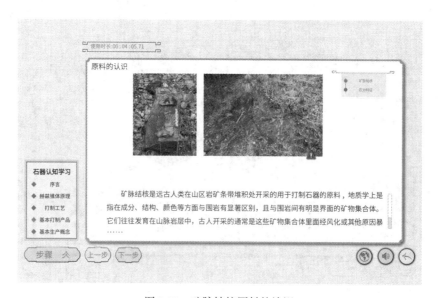

图1-22 矿脉结核原料的认识

点击"下一步"，可见对矿脉结核区分特征的解释(图1-23)。

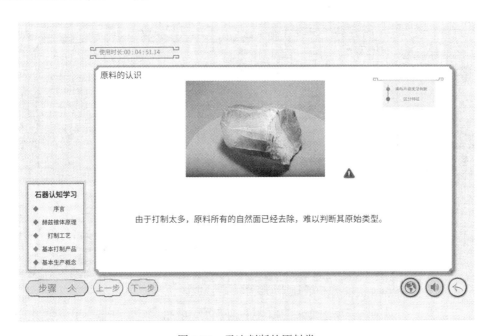

图1-23　矿脉结核的区分特征

(4)无法判断。

无法判断类型的原料是指那些由于打制太多，所有的自然面已经去除，难以判断其原始类型的原料(图1-24)。

图1-24　无法判断的原料类

点击"下一步"，可见对此类原料区分特征的解释(图 1-25)。

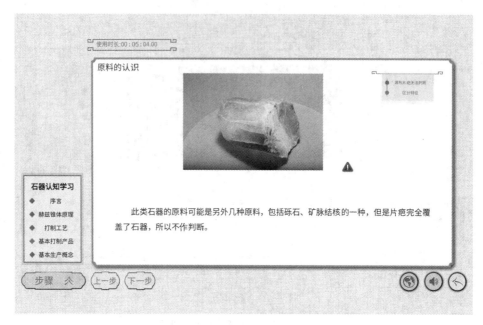

图 1-25　无法判断原料类的区分特征

依次点击"下一步"，进入两道学以致用的选择题及答案解析(图 1-26~图 1-27)。

图 1-26　原料认识的学以致用(1)

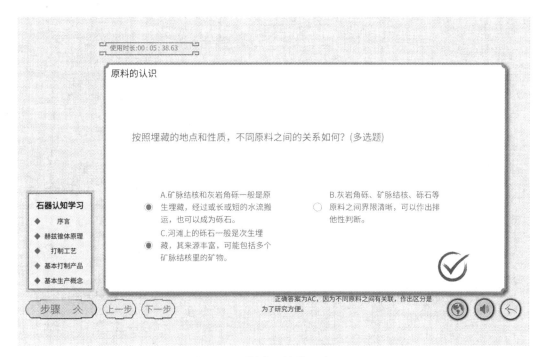

使用时长:00:05:38.63

原料的认识

按照埋藏的地点和性质,不同原料之间的关系如何?(多选题)

石器认知学习
◆ 序言
◆ 赫兹锥体原理
◆ 打制工艺
◆ 基本打制产品
◆ 基本生产概念

A.矿脉结核和灰岩角砾一般是原生埋藏,经过或长或短的水流搬运,也可以成为砾石。
C.河滩上的砾石一般是次生埋藏,其来源丰富,可能包括多个矿脉结核里的矿物。

B.灰岩角砾、矿脉结核、砾石等原料之间界限清晰,可以作出排他性判断。

正确答案为AC,因为不同原料之间有关联,作出区分是为了研究方便。

步骤 ∧   上一步   下一步

图1-27 原料认识的学以致用(2)

## 表面状态判别

### ◎ 实验原理:

结合岩石表面棱脊新鲜锐利的程度,考虑到野外旧石器埋藏的特点性质和肉眼观察的可操作性,我们常将石器表面状态分为三个等级:无明显磨蚀、中度磨蚀、重度磨蚀。

### ◎ 实验步骤:

依次点击"下一步",根据石器表面的状态学习如何判断其磨蚀程度。

(1)轻度磨蚀。

石器表面棱角新鲜锐利,打制形成的片疤看不出明显的冲磨、碰撞和风化作用,表明石器被废弃埋藏后没有经过明显的地质营力等因素的作用(图1-28)。

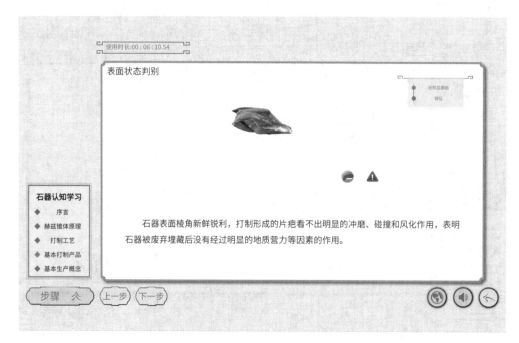

图 1-28　轻度磨蚀的定义

点击"下一步"，可见对轻度磨蚀特征的解释(图 1-29)。

图 1-29　轻度磨蚀的特征

（2）中度磨蚀。

石器表面棱角可见，但不太新鲜锐利，打制形成的片疤可见一定程度的冲磨、碰撞和风化作用，表明石器被废弃埋藏后经过了短时间的地质营力等因素的作用（图1-30）。

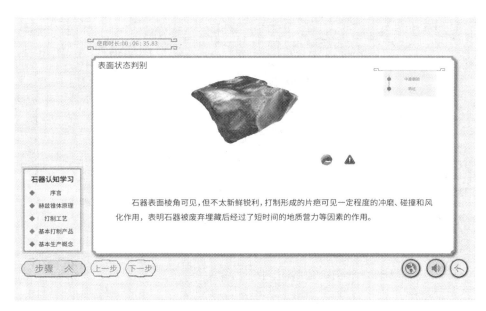

图1-30　中度磨蚀的定义

点击"下一步"，可见对中度磨蚀特征的解释（图1-31）。

图1-31　中度磨蚀的特征

(3)重度磨蚀。

石器表面棱角已不凸出，变得圆钝，打制形成的片疤也被明显磨平，表明石器被废弃埋藏后经过了很长时间的地质营力等因素的作用(图1-32)。

图 1-32 重度磨蚀的定义

点击"下一步"，可见对重度磨蚀特征的解释(图1-33)。

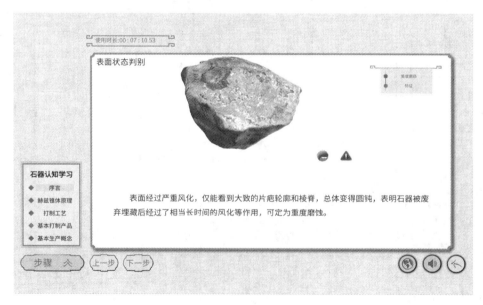

图 1-33 重度磨蚀的特征

点击"下一步",进入一道学以致用的选择题及答案解析(图1-34)。

图 1-34 表面状态判别的学以致用

## 石片的认知学习

◎ 实验原理:

通过文字解释、图片或者三维模型来学习石片的技术要素。

◎ 实验步骤:

进入初识石片界面后,依次点击"下一步",根据照片以及转动三维模型来学习石片的定义、石片台面的分类、石片背面的分类、石片的摆放定位、石片的测量、石片或片疤打击方向的判别。学习完基本概念后完成学以致用的选择题。

(1)石片的定义。

石片在广义上是从石质母体上剥离下的一部分碎片,这个母体可以是石核或工具。由于赫兹锥体原理的作用,石片具有相似的可以辨认的特征,包括台面、打击点、打击泡、同心波、背面、腹面、石片角、打击方向、放射线、同心波(图1-35~图1-44)。

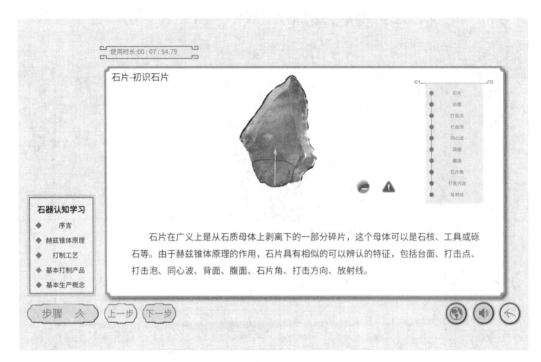

图 1-35　初识石片

图 1-36　石片台面的定义

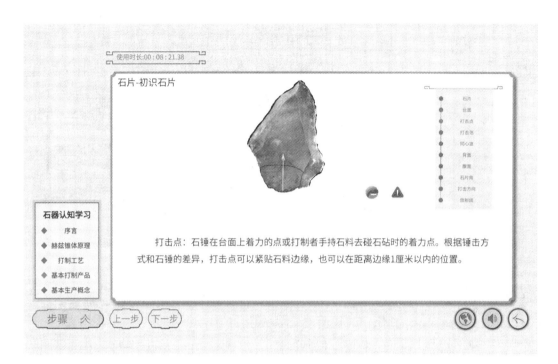

图1-37 石片打击点的概念

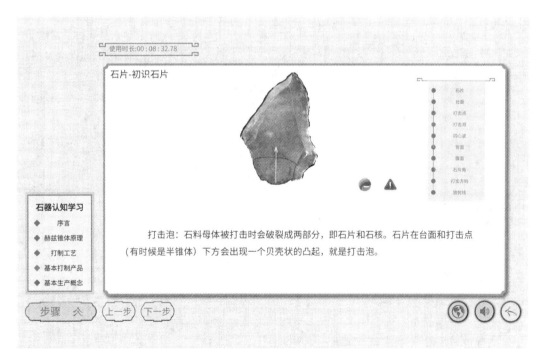

图1-38 石片打击泡的概念

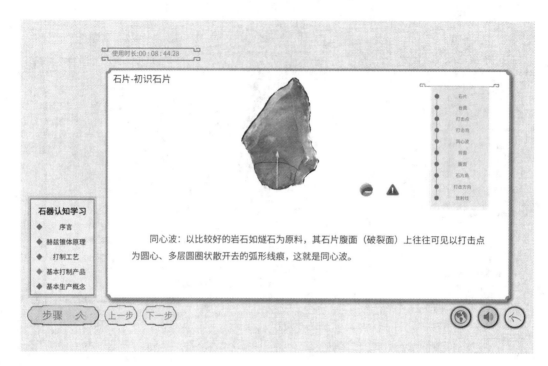

图 1-39 石片同心波的概念

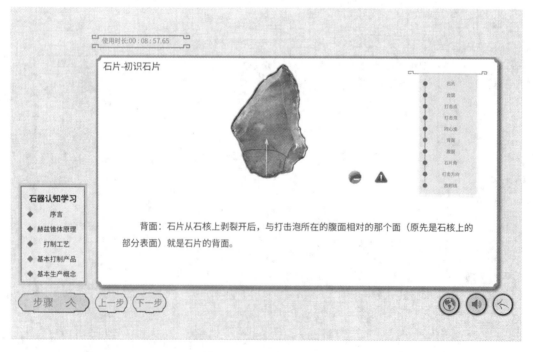

图 1-40 石片背面的概念

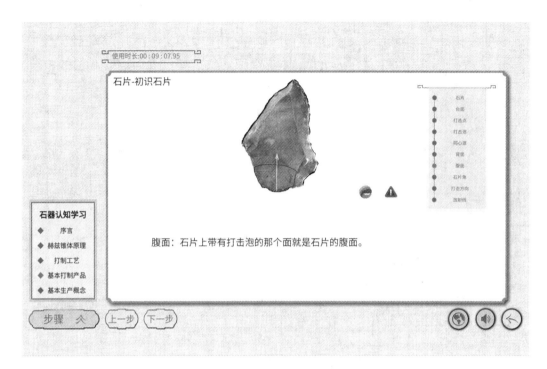

图 1-41　石片腹面的概念

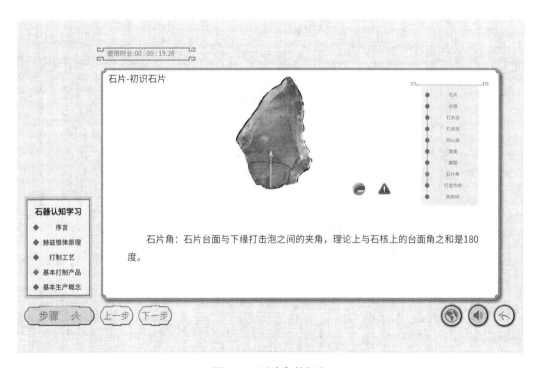

图 1-42　石片角的概念

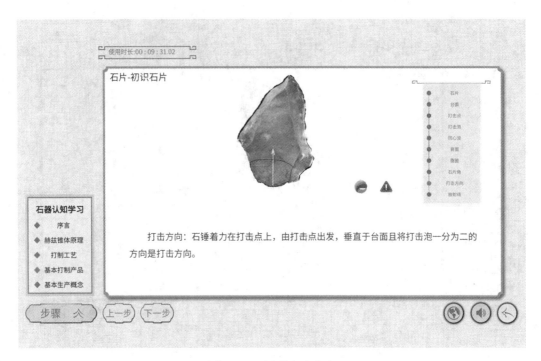

图 1-43　石片的打击方向

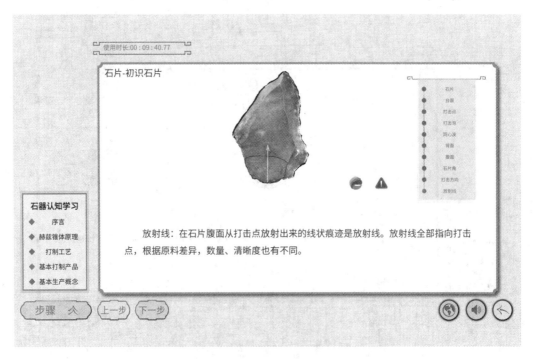

图 1-44　石片的放射线

（2）石片台面的分类。

石片台面包括自然面、单个片疤、二面台面、多面台面、宪兵帽状、隆凸状、针眼状、线状等类型。依次点击"下一步"，完成对这些类型定义的学习（图1-45~图1-52）。

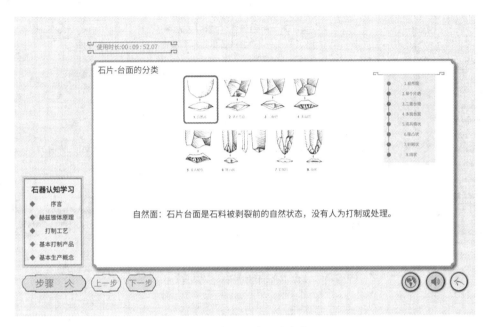

图 1-45　台面的类型之自然面

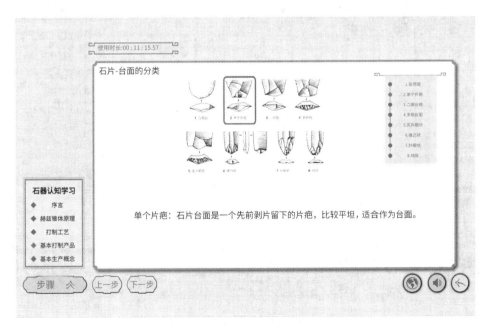

图 1-46　台面的类型之单个片疤

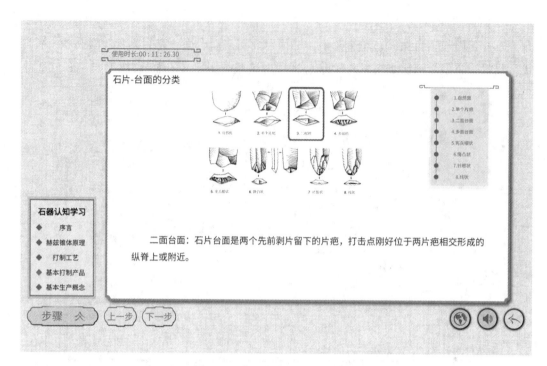

图 1-47　台面的类型之二面台面

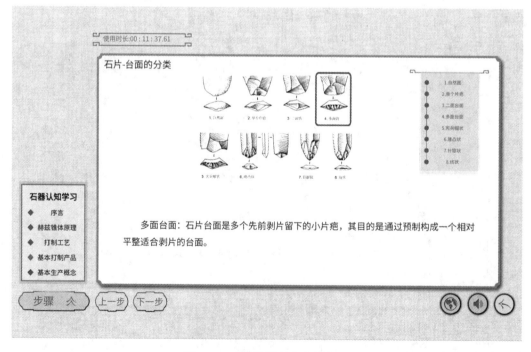

图 1-48　台面的类型之多面台面

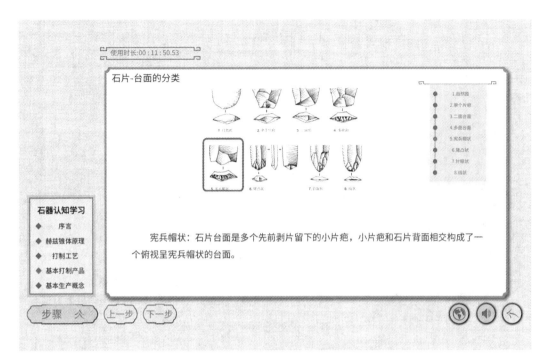

图 1-49 台面的类型之宪兵帽状

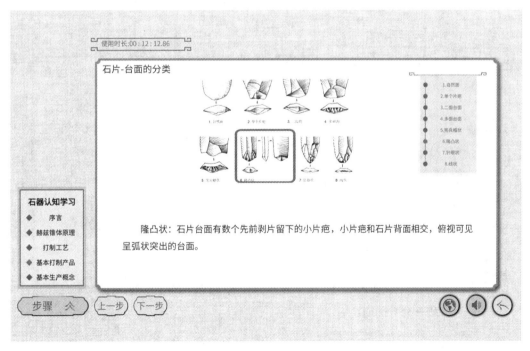

图 1-50 台面的类型之隆凸状

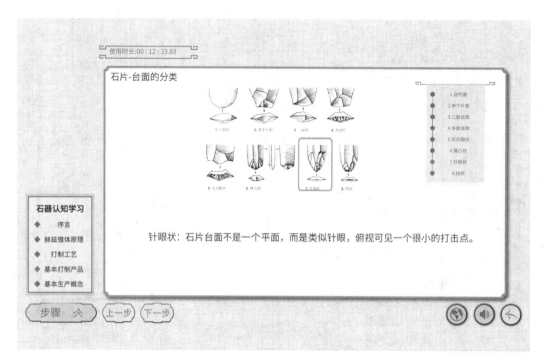

图 1-51  台面的类型之针眼状

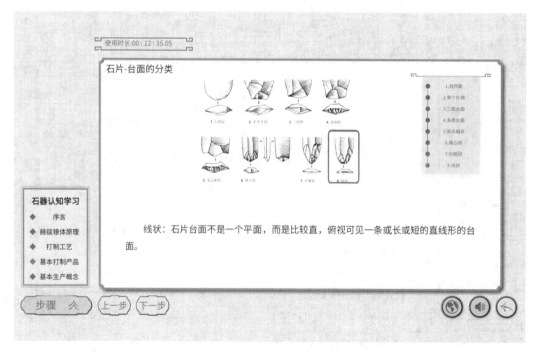

图 1-52  台面的类型之线状

点击"下一步"，进入学以致用，回答选择题(图1-53)。

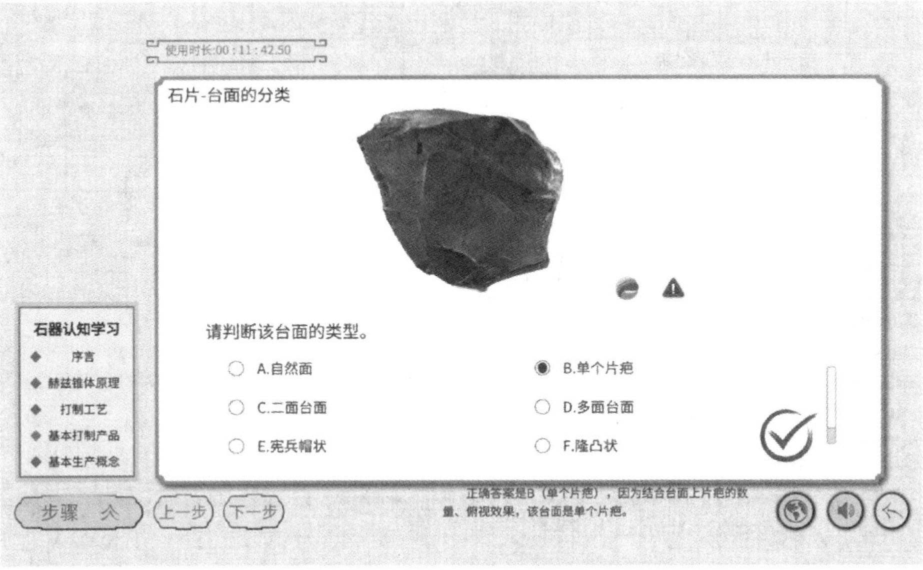

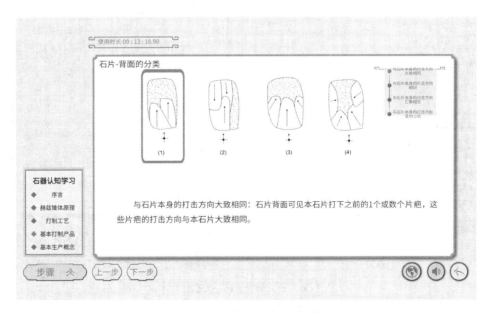

图1-53　台面类型的判断

(3)石片背面的分类。

石片背面有四种类型，分别是与石片本身的打击方向大致相同、与石片本身的打击方向相对、与石片本身的打击方向汇聚相交、与石片本身的打击方向呈向心式。依次点击"下一步"，完成对这些类型定义的学习(图1-54~图1-57)。

图1-54　石片背面的类型之同向式

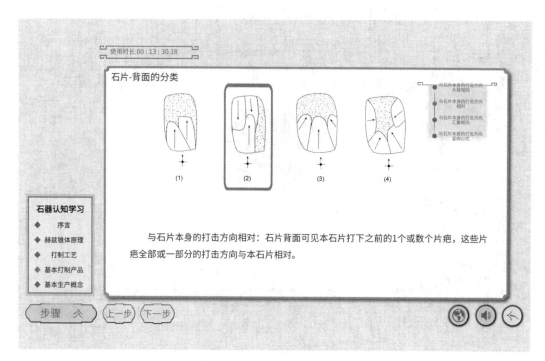

图 1-55　石片背面的类型之对向式

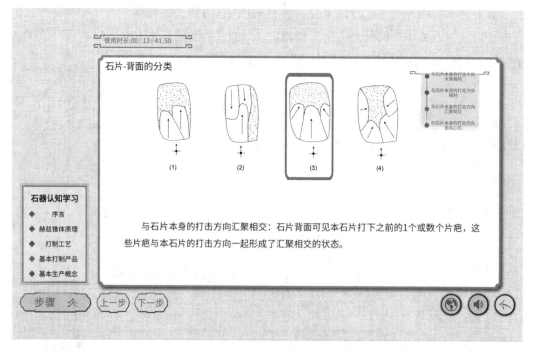

图 1-56　石片背面的类型之汇聚式

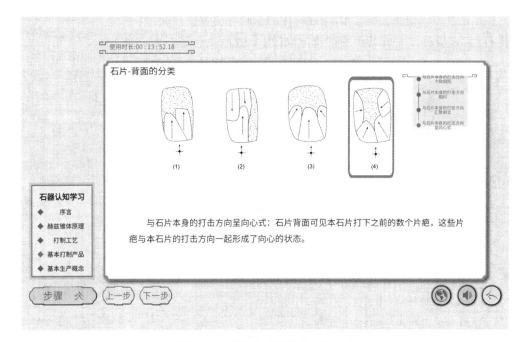

图 1-57　石片背面的类型之向心式

点击"下一步"，进入学以致用，回答选择题(图 1-58)。

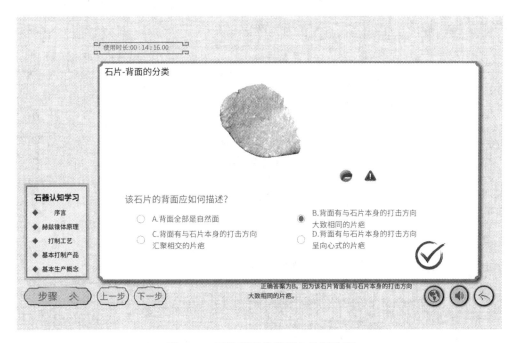

图 1-58　石片背面的类型之学以致用

（4）石片的摆放定位。

根据前面学习到的知识，请练习石片的正确摆放定位。通过长按鼠标右键，抓取并旋转石片 3D 模型，完成石片的摆放定位（图 1-59）。

图 1-59　石片的摆放定位

点击"下一步"，进入学以致用，通过鼠标抓取旋转石器 3D 模型来完成该石片正确的摆放定位（图 1-60）。

图 1-60　石片摆放定位的学以致用

（5）石片或石片片疤的测量。

使用页面右侧工具栏里的游标卡尺，放大或缩小按钮来测量标本的长度和宽度，并填入弹出来的对话框中。同时学习石片的近端、远端、中部、左侧边、右侧边等描述性术语的含义（图1-61~图1-67）。

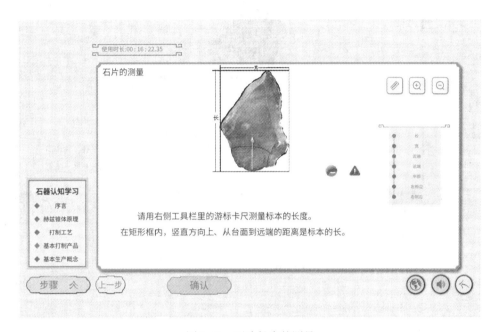

图 1-61　石片长度的测量

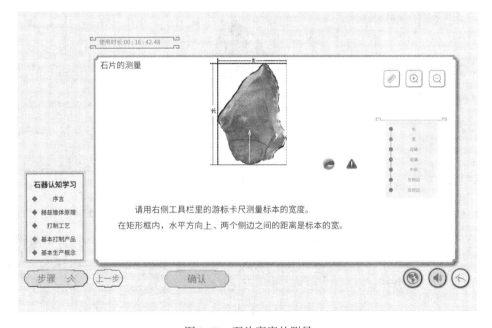

图 1-62　石片宽度的测量

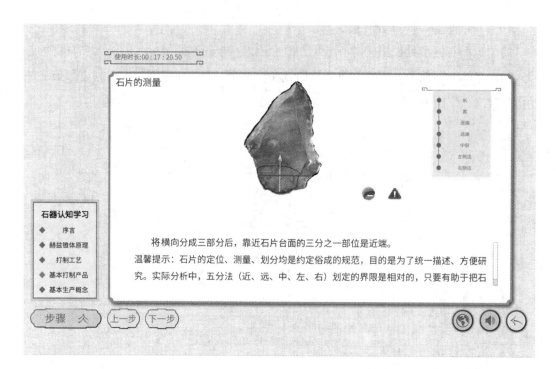

图 1-63　石片的近端

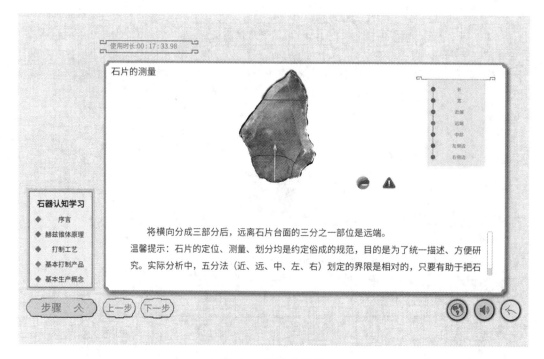

图 1-64　石片的远端

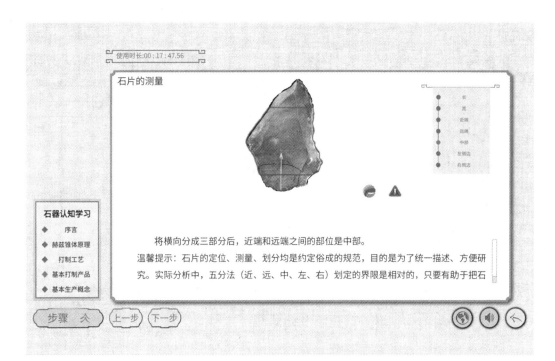

图 1-65　石片的中部

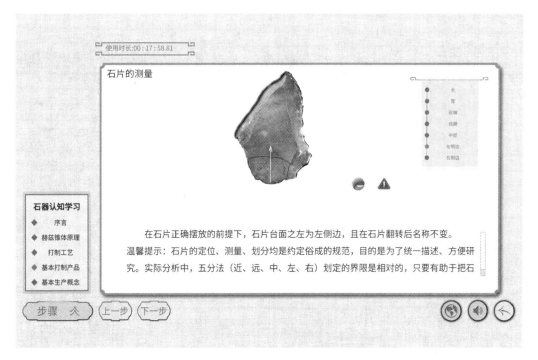

图 1-66　石片的左侧边

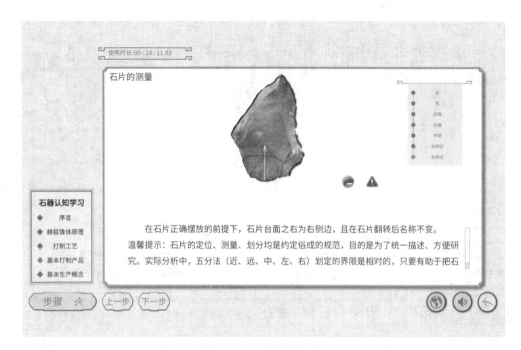

图 1-67　石片的右侧边

点击"下一步"，进入学以致用的测试题(图 1-68~图 1-69)。

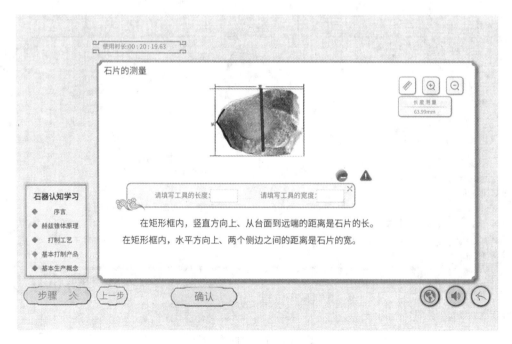

图 1-68　测量石片的学以致用(1)

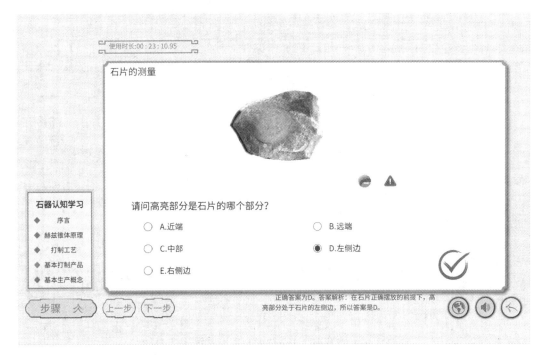

图 1-69 测量石片的学以致用（2）

(6)石片或片疤打击方向的判别。

台面可见时，与台面垂直的方向就是打击方向；打击泡可见时，从打击点出发，将打击泡一分为二的方向就是石片的打击方向；同心波可见时，两条同心波的弦的中垂线的相交点是打击点，从打击点出发，结合石片的整体形态判断的方向就是石片的打击方向；放射线可见时，所有放射线指向的点是打击点，从打击点出发，结合石片的整体形态判断的方向就是石片的打击方向；反泡可见时，与打击泡类似，反泡的近端是打击点，从打击点出发，将反泡一分为二的方向就是片疤的打击方向。依次点击"下一步"，理解各技术要素所具有的指示性意义(图1-70~图1-74)。

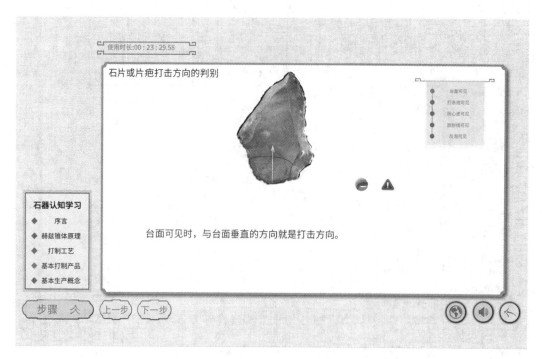

图 1-70　石片或片疤打击方向的判别因素之台面可见时

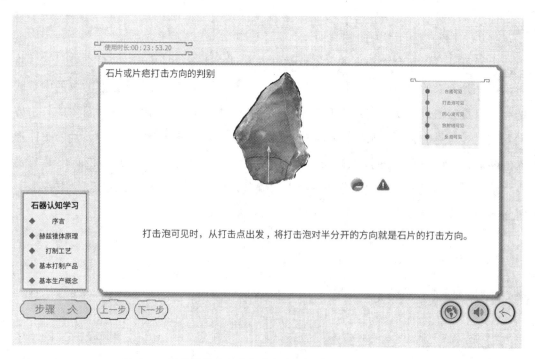

图 1-71　石片或片疤打击方向的判别因素之打击泡可见时

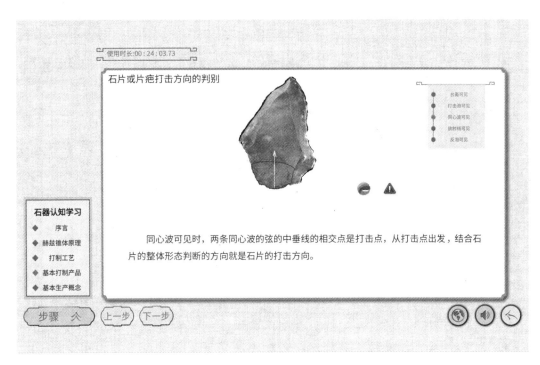

图 1-72 石片或片疤打击方向的判别因素之同心波可见时

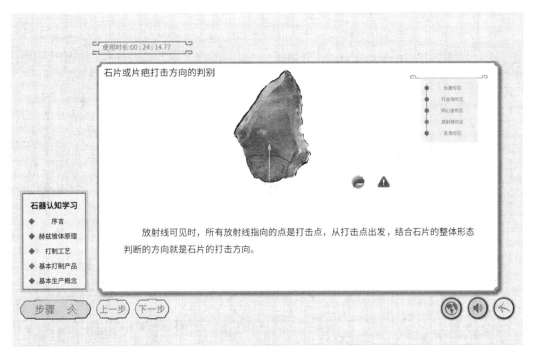

图 1-73 石片或片疤打击方向的判别因素之放射线可见时

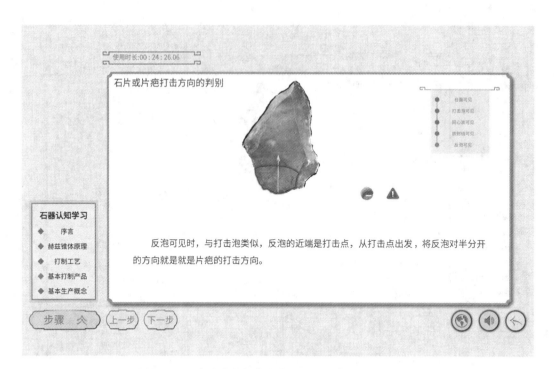

图 1-74　石片或片疤打击方向的判别因素之反泡可见时

点击"下一步"，进入学以致用选择题的练习（图 1-75）。

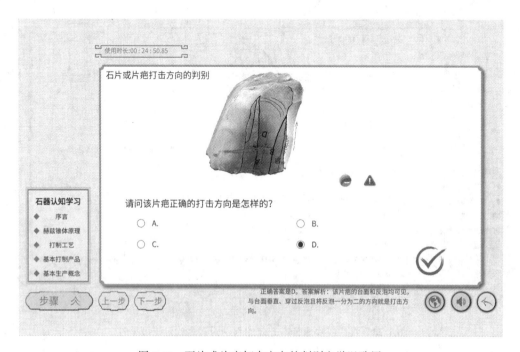

图 1-75　石片或片疤打击方向的判别之学以致用

## 🗐 石核的认知学习

### ◎ 实验原理:

通过石器照片或者三维模型来学习石核的技术要素。

### ◎ 实验步骤:

进入初识石核界面后,依次点击"下一步",了解石核表面的技术特征,包括台面、打击点、反泡、纵脊、台面角、剥坯面、打击方向、放射线、同心波等。同时对石核的摆放定位、石核台面的判定、石核片疤的测量进行深入学习并完成学以致用的练习。

(1)石核的定义。

考古遗址中所见的石核一般是剥坯完成后剩下的石块。由于赫兹锥体原理的作用,石核表面会产生可以辨认的一些特征,包括台面、打击点、反泡、纵脊、台面角、剥坯面、打击方向、放射线、同心波等。理论上石核与石片本属于同一个母体石块,二者的区别在于,石片台面下方一般会有一个突出的打击泡,而石核上对应的位置是一个凹陷,即反泡(图1-76~图1-85)。

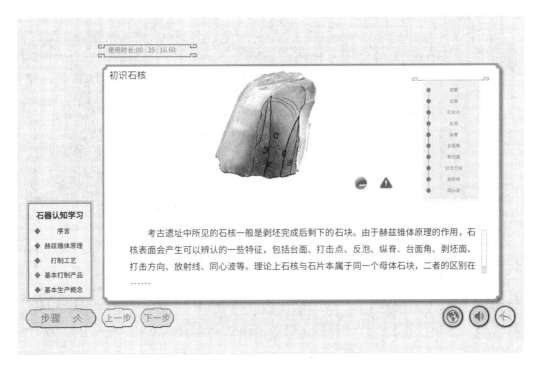

图 1-76　初识石核的技术特征

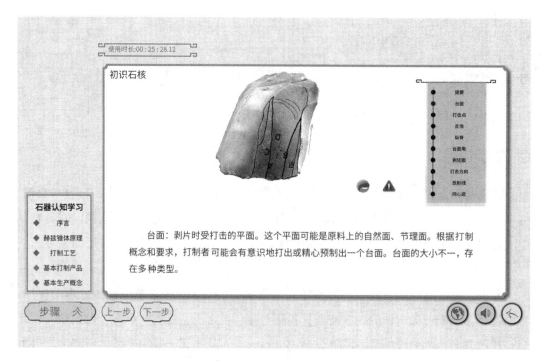

图 1-77　石核台面的定义

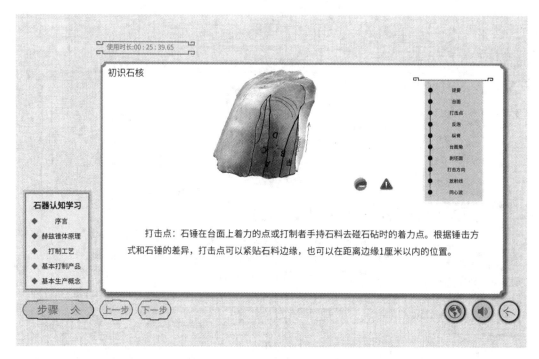

图 1-78　石核打击点的定义

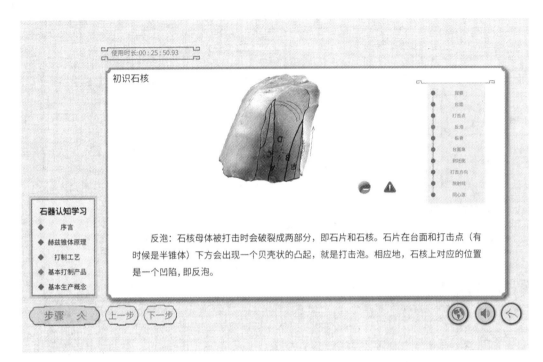

图 1-79　石核反泡的定义

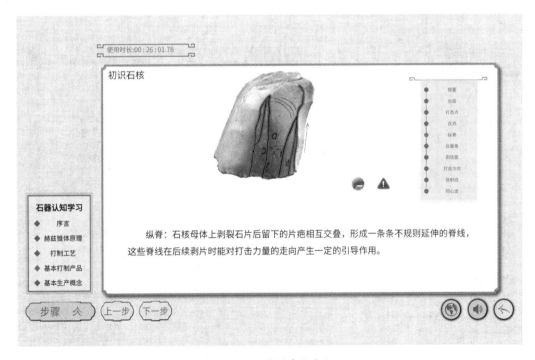

图 1-80　石核纵脊的定义

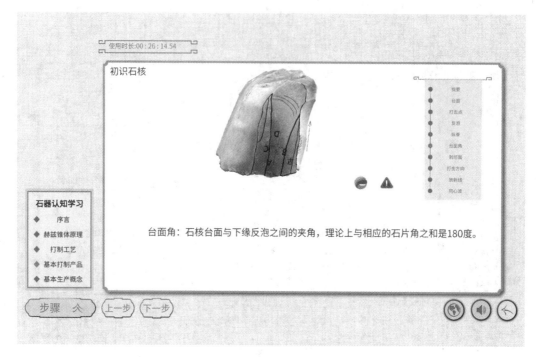

图 1-81  石核台面角的定义

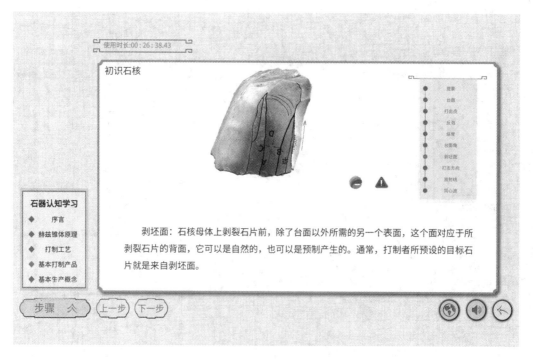

图 1-82  石核剥坯面的定义

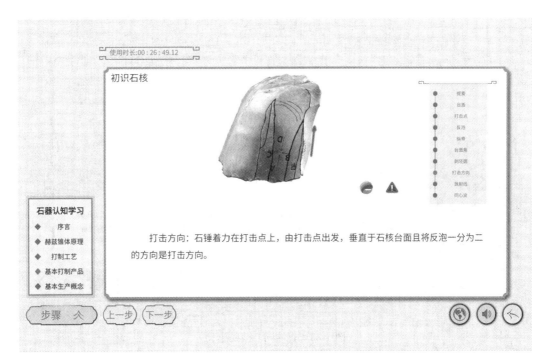

图1-83 石核打击方向的定义

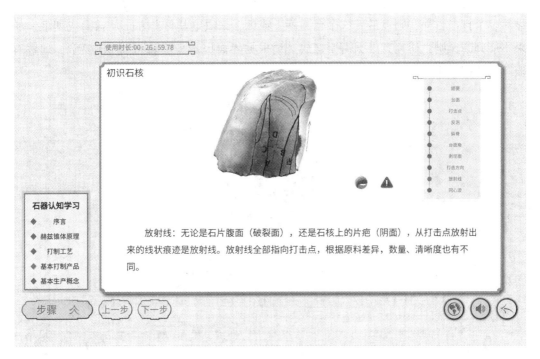

图1-84 石核放射线的定义

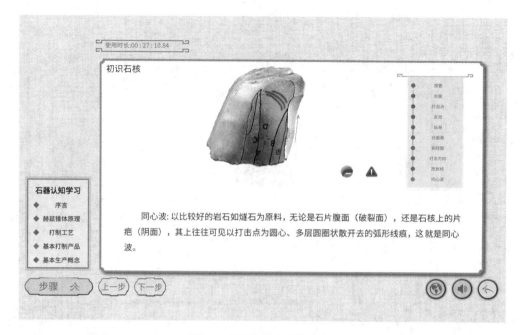

图 1-85　石核同心波的定义

(2)石核的摆放定位。

石核的摆放定位没有特定规则,取决于研究者对石核剥坯过程的分析,如果能判断最后一个打击台面,则以最后这个台面朝下或朝上来决定其打击方向是朝上或朝下。如果不能判断,则由研究者根据需要摆放。请根据界面提示来旋转石器 3D 模型,理解石核一般的摆放定位规则(图 1-86)。

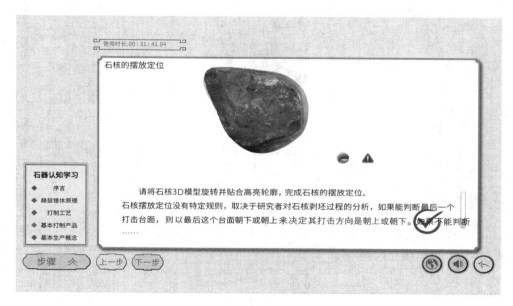

图 1-86　石核的摆放定位

（3）石核台面的判定。

石核的台面类型分为自然面、节理面、先前剥片的片疤和人工预制。请依次点击"下一步"，完成各台面类型的学习（图1-87～图1-90）。

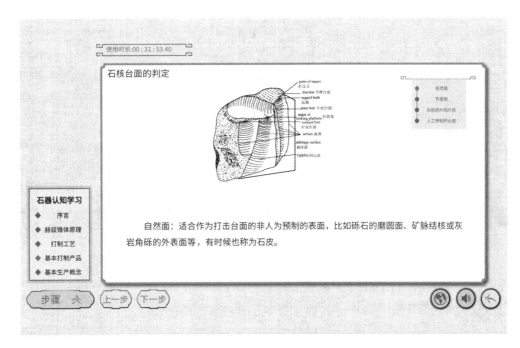

图 1-87　石核台面的类型之自然面

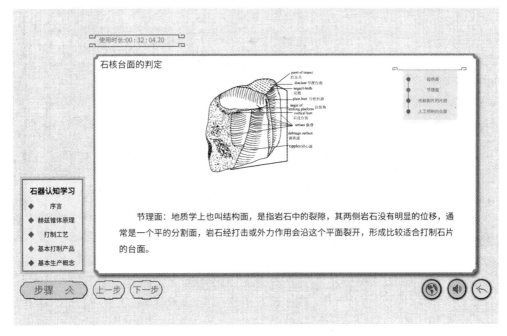

图 1-88　石核台面的类型之节理面

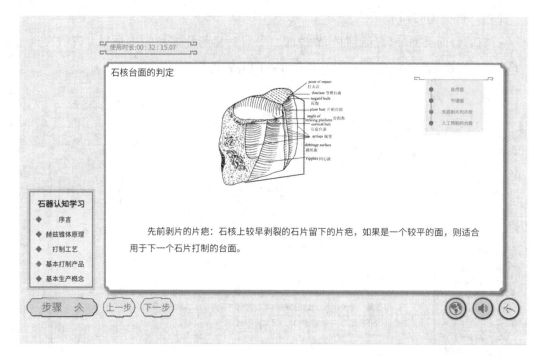

图 1-89　石核台面的类型之先前剥片的片疤

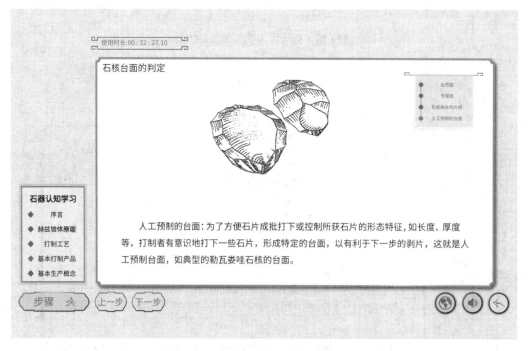

图 1-90　石核台面的类型之人工预制的台面

点击"下一步"，进入学以致用的测试题(图1-91)。

图 1-91 石核台面类型判定的学以致用

(4)石核片疤的测量。

调整图中石核 3D 模型的摆放，将预先标注的长方形调整到正对观察者的位置，该长方形所框定的范围即为待测量片疤的范围。根据提示，测量该片疤的长度和宽度，并按照系统提示填写数据(图1-92)。

图 1-92 石核片疤的测量

点击"下一步"，进入学以致用的测试题(图 1-93)。

图 1-93　石核的学以致用

点击"下一步"，完成学以致用的测量填空题(图 1-94)。

图 1-94　石核片疤的测量之学以致用

## 1.2.5 基本的生产概念

◎ **实验步骤：**

点击"下一步"，结合3D动画和文字解说理解什么是生产概念以及世界旧石器技术演化中的两种生产概念：剥坯和修型(图1-95)。

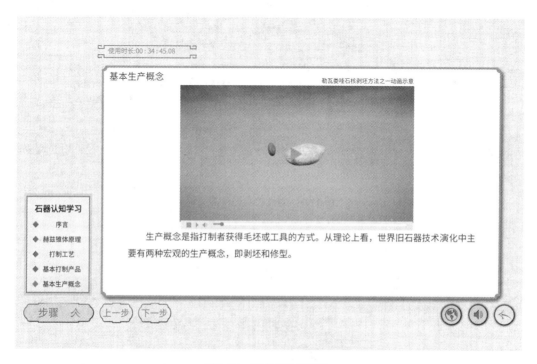

图1-95 基本的生产概念

(1)学习剥坯概念，点击"下一步"，在阅读文字的同时观看3D动画演示视频。播放完毕后可以点击"重播"按钮进行重播，以加深理解剥坯的概念(图1-96)。

(2)学习修型概念，点击"下一步"，在阅读文字的同时观看3D动画演示视频。播放完毕后可以点击"重播"按钮进行重播，以加深理解修型的概念(图1-97)。

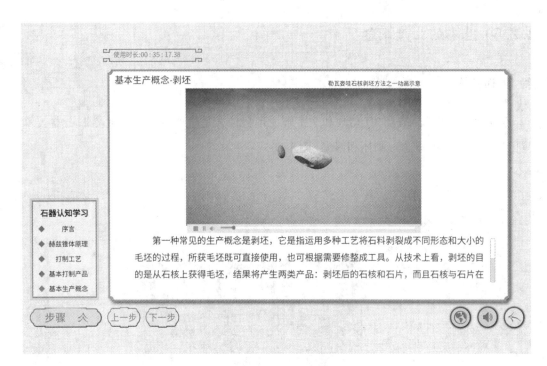

图 1-96　剥坯概念的学习

图 1-97　修型概念的学习

## 1.3 石器拼合实验

从"石器认知学习"模块退出，选择"石器拼合实验"模块，进入序言，了解石器拼合分析的基本概念。

### 1.3.1 序言

拼合分析是通过将不同的石制品根据"表面接合"和/或"厚度接合"的方式，从碎片拼成一个整体，从而理解石器打制先后顺序和过程、复原遗址结构和埋藏过程、重建人类活动空间分布以及遗址形成过程的一种研究方法(图 1-98)。

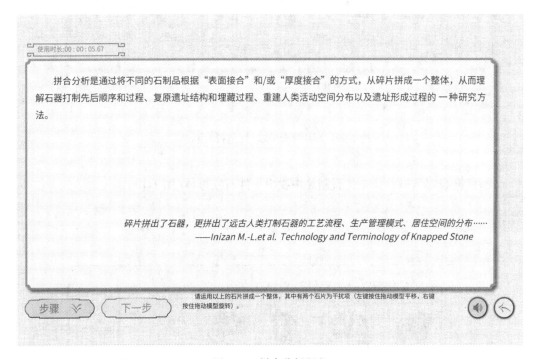

图 1-98 拼合分析释义

### 1.3.2 简单拼合实验

◎ **实验步骤：**

点击"下一步"，进入简单拼合实验的环节，从 10 件石制品中根据观察挑选颜色、质地类似的 7 件石制品，观察石片上的片疤和形态，完成拼合实验。

（1）点击放大镜对所有石制品进行观察；根据观察结果，从 10 件碎片里面挑选 7 件颜色、质地类似的石制品(图 1-99)。

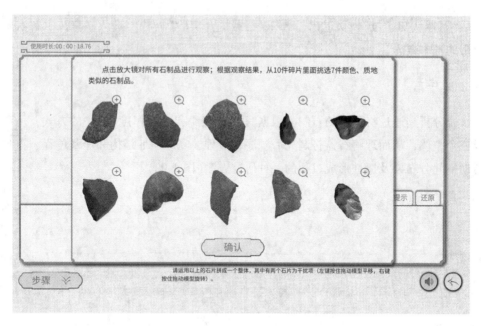

图 1-99　石片拼合的步骤(选择石制品)

（2）根据观察结果，从 7 件石制品中找出 1 件石核母体(图 1-100)。

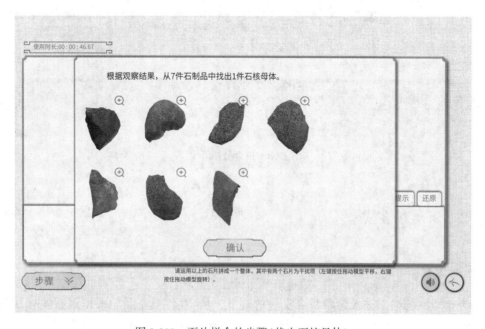

图 1-100　石片拼合的步骤(找出石核母体)

（3）通过鼠标抓取、移动石片和旋转石核母体，完成拼合（图1-101）。

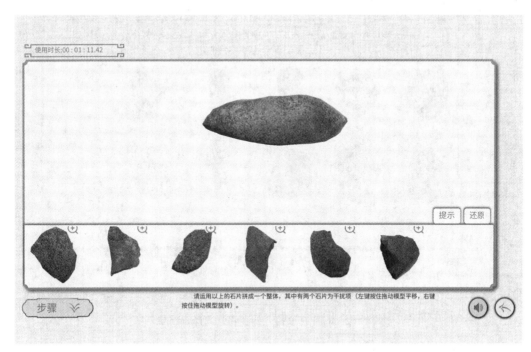

图 1-101　石片拼合的步骤（移动石片完成拼合）

### 1.3.3　复杂拼合实验

📑 **实验原理：无**

◎ **实验步骤：**

点击"下一步"，进入复杂拼合实验的环节，从 35 件石制品中根据观察挑选颜色、质地类似的 32 件石制品，然后找出石核母体，拖动石片完成拼合实验。拼合完成后系统会根据时长给出分数。

（1）点击放大镜对所有石制品进行观察；根据观察结果，从 35 件碎片里面挑选 32 件颜色、质地类似的石制品（图1-102）。

（2）根据观察结果，从 32 件石制品中找出 1 件石核母体（图1-103）。

（3）依次将石片拖拽到石核上进行拼合（图1-104）。

（4）完成拼合之后，点击返回按钮，回到"探索之旅"，进入"石器技术阅读"模块。

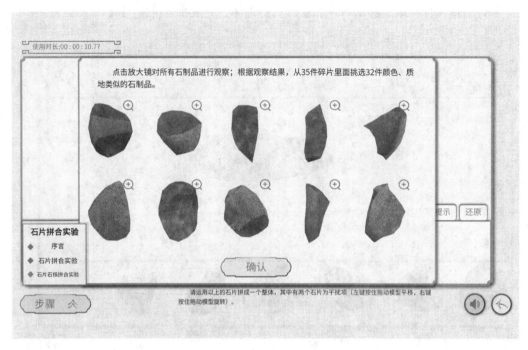

图 1-102　石片石核拼合的步骤之选择石制品

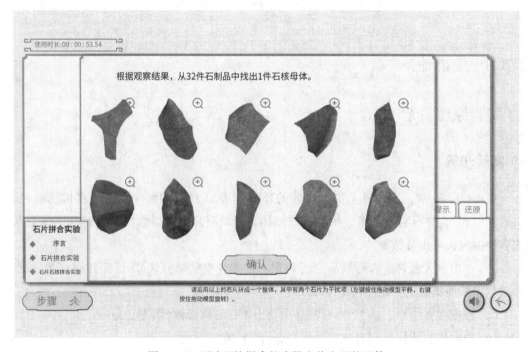

图 1-103　石片石核拼合的步骤之找出石核母体

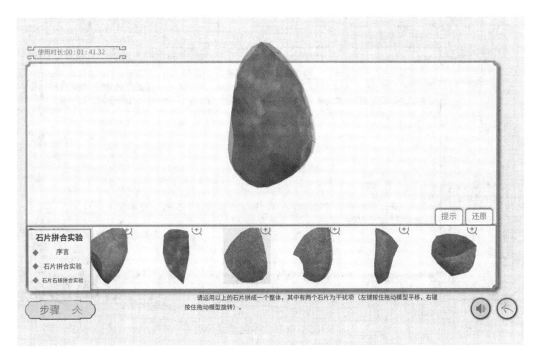

图 1-104　石片石核拼合的步骤之移动石片进行拼合

## 1.4　石器技术阅读

选择"石器技术阅读"模块，进入序言，简单了解石器技术阅读的目的和意义。

### 1.4.1　序言

透石见人，是旧石器考古学的首要目标。技术学研究和打制实验共同表明，打制者在制作石器的过程中都运用了或长或短、或复杂或简单的操作链，并受到一定打制想法的支配，理解打制者的想法就需要进行技术阅读。掌握了石器技术阅读，就掌握了一套规则，可以系统、科学地对古人类的行为和认知进行观察、解构和感知(图 1-105)。

### 1.4.2　单件石器的技术阅读

◎ **实验步骤：**

依次点击"下一步"或侧边栏的标题，进入单件石器的技术阅读。

(1)原料的认识。

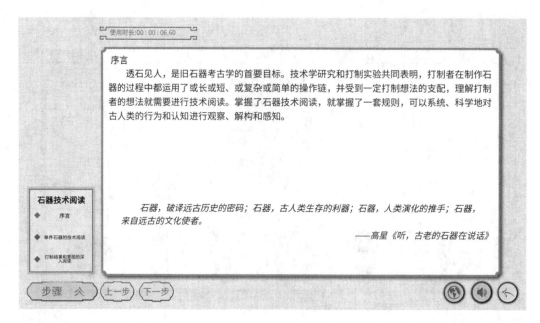

图 1-105　石器技术阅读之序言

通过之前所学知识，转动、缩放石器三维模型，判断石器的原料。系统将判断答案正误，并给予解析(图 1-106)。

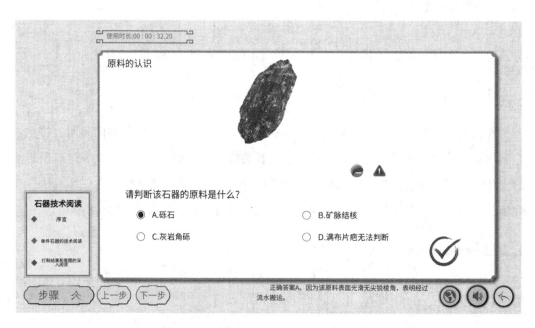

图 1-106　单件石器技术阅读之原料的认识

（2）表面状态的判别。

通过之前所学知识，转动、缩放石器三维模型，判断石器的磨损状态。系统将判断答案正误，并给予解析（图1-107）。

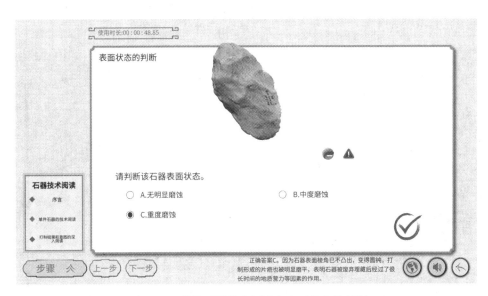

图1-107 单件石器技术阅读之表面状态的判别

（3）片疤打击方向的判别。

通过之前所学知识，转动、缩放石器三维模型，判断石器片疤的打击方向。系统将判断答案正误，并给予解析（图1-108）。

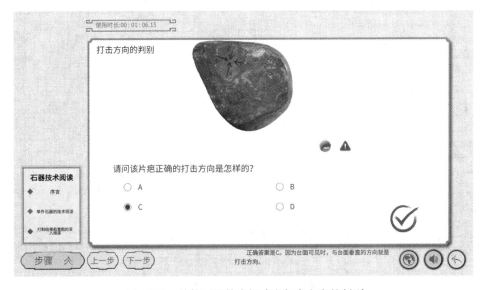

图1-108 单件石器技术阅读之打击方向的判别

（4）片疤打击顺序的判别。

点击"下一步"，学习片疤打击顺序判别的依据。根据片疤风化磨蚀程度比较、相交片疤的完整度、片疤相交处棱脊的刺手程度、时间顺序不可逆的逻辑原则、同向片疤深度差异、相交片疤反泡的可见度、相交片疤放射线的可见度来判断片疤打击顺序的先后（图 1-109~图 1-114）。

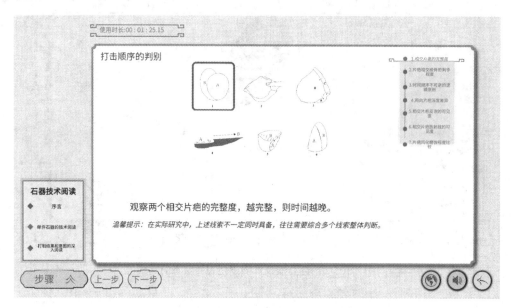

图 1-109　片疤打击顺序的判别标准（1）

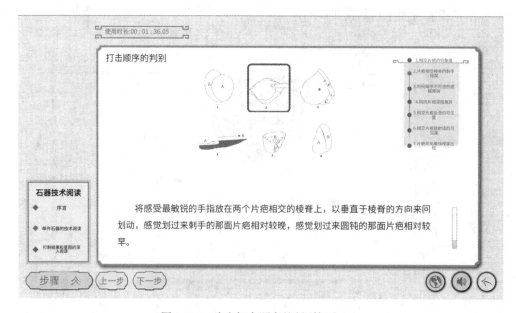

图 1-110　片疤打击顺序的判别标准（2）

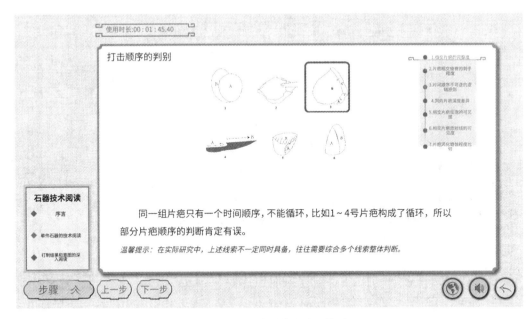

图 1-111 片疤打击顺序的判别标准(3)

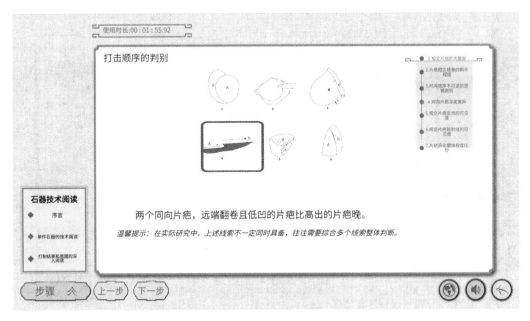

图 1-112 片疤打击顺序的判别标准(4)

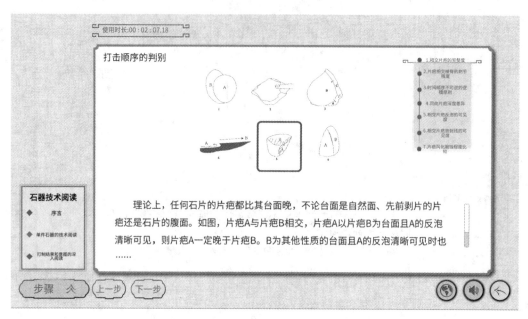

图 1-113　片疤打击顺序的判别标准(5)

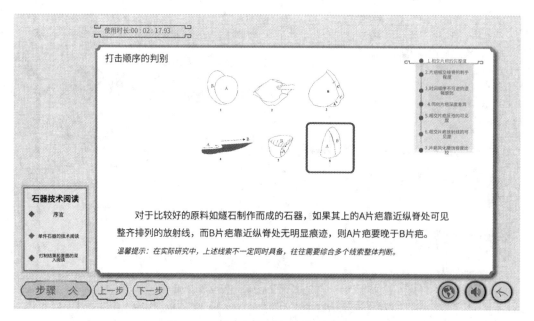

图 1-114　片疤打击顺序的判别标准(6)

点击"下一步"，进入学以致用的判断题(图 1-115)。

图 1-115 片疤打击顺序的判别之学以致用

## 1.4.3 打制结果和意图的深入阅读

◎ 实验步骤：

(1)石核剥坯体系的判断。

点击"下一步"，进入"打制结果和意图的深入阅读"。首先进入石核剥坯体系的判断，通过转动、缩放石器三维模型，然后判断台面、两侧凸度、远端凸度，最后再进行石核剥坯体系的判断。总共四小题，学生在思考中了解判断石核剥坯体系的思路。本知识点以简单石核剥坯、Levallois 石核剥坯以及石叶石核剥坯三种剥坯体系为例供学习(图 1-116～图 1-126)。

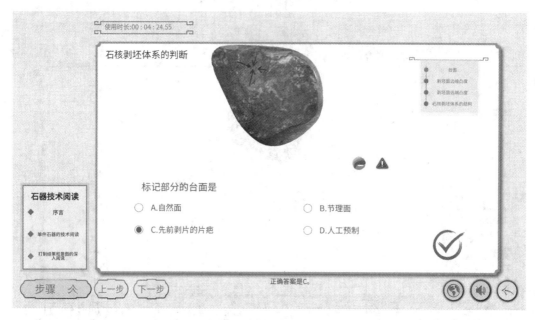

图 1-116　石核剥坯体系的学以致用(1)

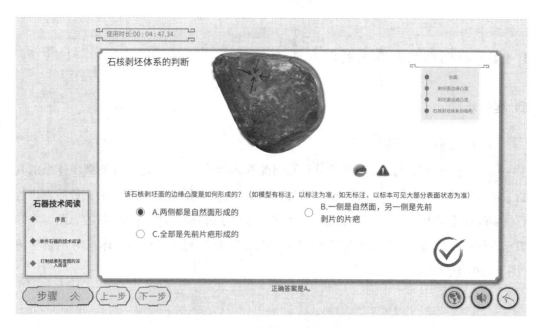

图 1-117　石核剥坯体系的学以致用(2)

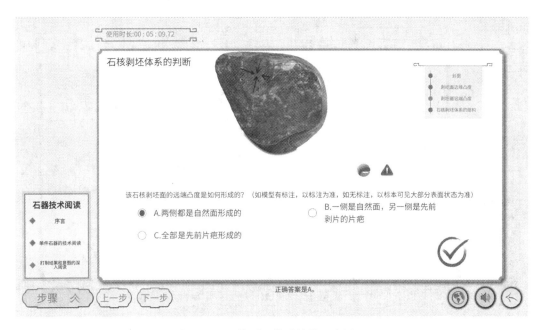

图 1-118　石核剥坯体系的学以致用(3)

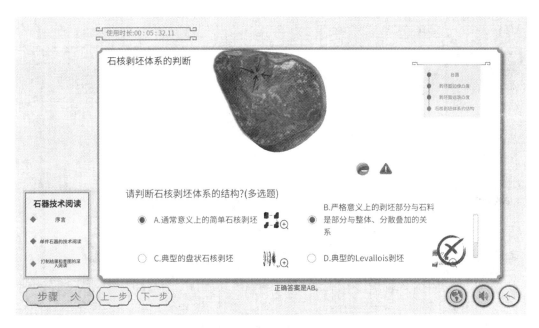

图 1-119　石核剥坯体系的学以致用(4)

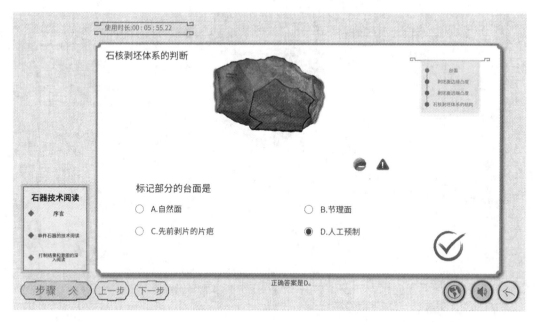

图 1-120　石核剥坯体系的学以致用(5)

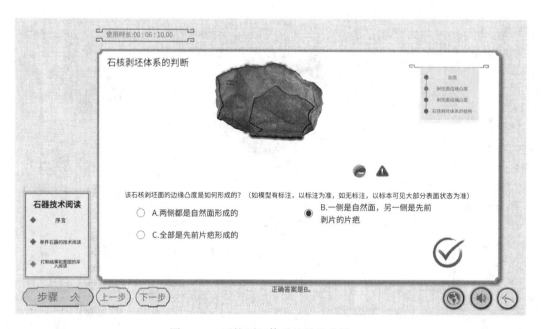

图 1-121　石核剥坯体系的学以致用(6)

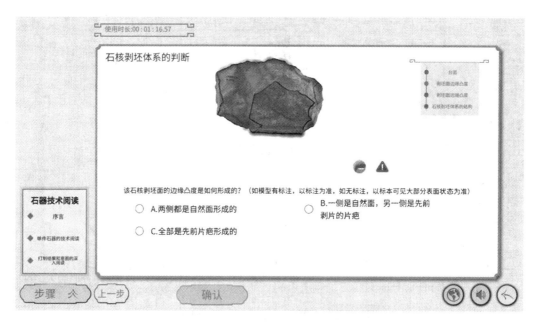

图 1-122 石核剥坯体系的学以致用(7)

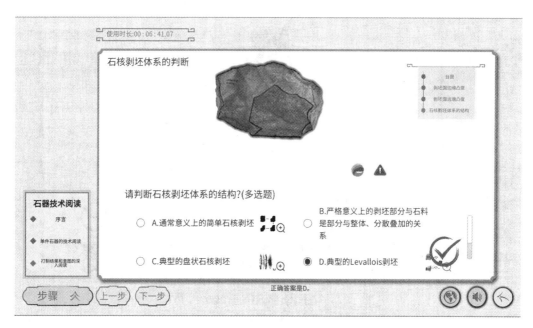

图 1-123 石核剥坯体系的学以致用(8)

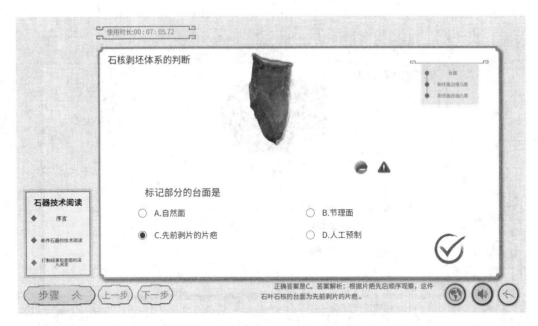

图 1-124　石核剥坯体系的学以致用（9）

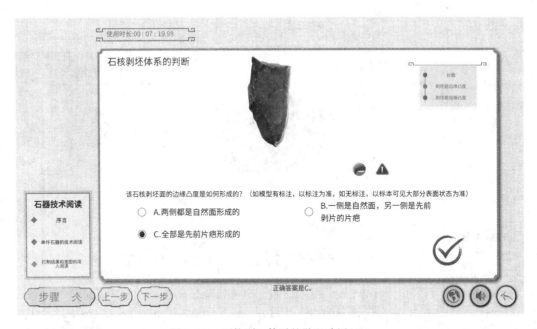

图 1-125　石核剥坯体系的学以致用（10）

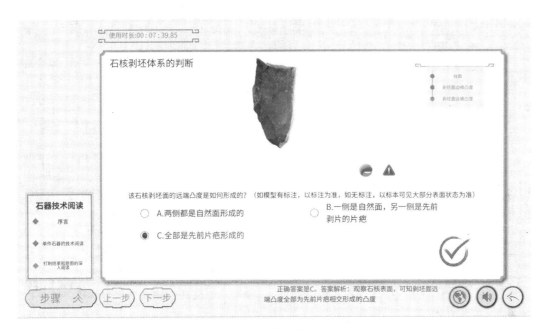

图 1-126　石核剥坯体系的学以致用(11)

(2)修型工具的技术-功能阅读之摆放定位。

点击"下一步",进入"摆放定位"。学生学习修型工具的摆放定位知识后,按住鼠标右键,对石器模型进行旋转,直到将其旋转至正确的摆放定位(图 1-127~图 1-128)。

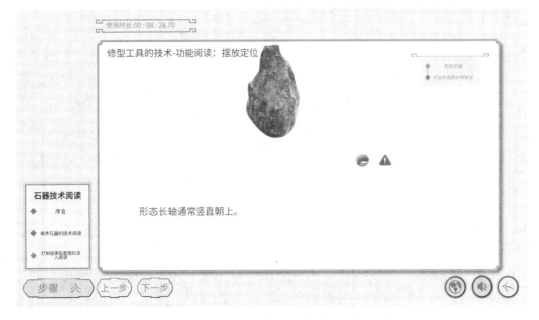

图 1-127　修型工具的技术-功能阅读之摆放定位

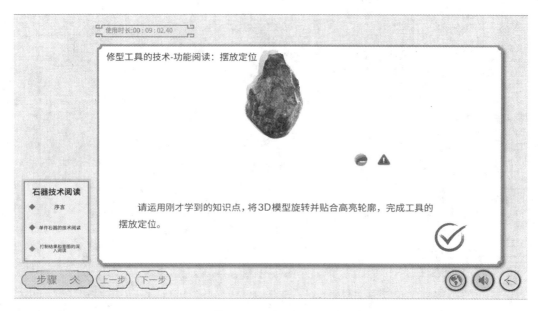

图 1-128  修型工具的摆放定位之学以致用

（3）修型工具的技术-功能阅读之尺寸分析。

点击"下一步"，进入"尺寸分析"。点击右侧工具栏的直尺按钮，可使用尺子对工具的长、宽、厚进行测量，并填入对话框的空白处，系统会在一定误差范围内判断正误。根据测量结果，学生计算后得出形态类型。本知识点提供两面器和单面器供学习（图 1-129）。

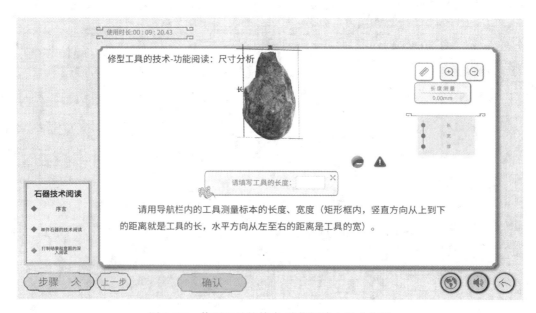

图 1-129  修型工具的技术-功能阅读之尺寸分析

点击"下一步"，进入学以致用(图1-130~图1-131)。

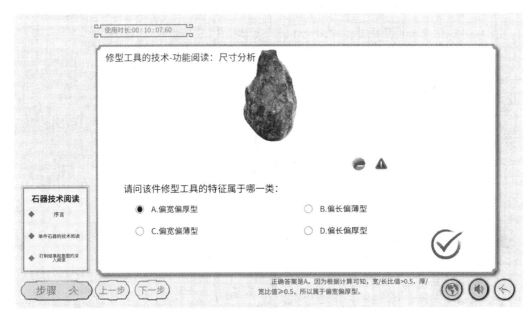

图1-130　修型工具尺寸分析的学以致用(1)

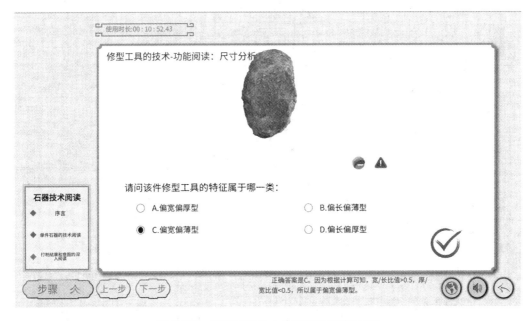

图1-131　修型工具尺寸分析的学以致用(2)

(4)修型工具的技术-功能阅读之结构观察。

点击"下一步",进入"结构观察"。点击右边工具栏的截面工具,可对石器模型进行任意位置和方向的截断,学生可任意旋转模型观察石器的截面形态,回答相关问题。本知识点提供两个不同的两面器供学习(图 1-132~图 1-135)。

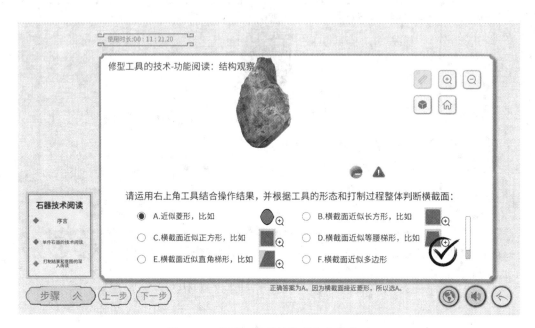

图 1-132 修型工具的结构观察之横截面

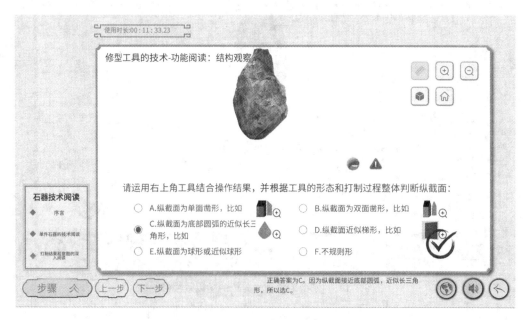

图 1-133 修型工具的结构观察之纵截面

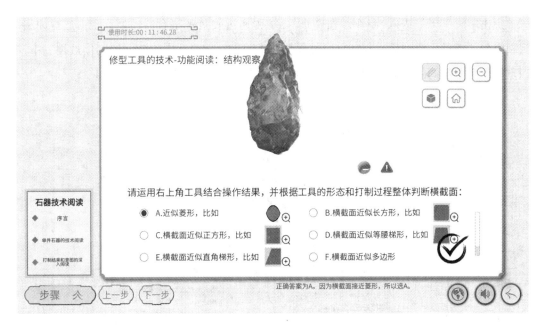

图 1-134 修型工具的横截面观察之学以致用

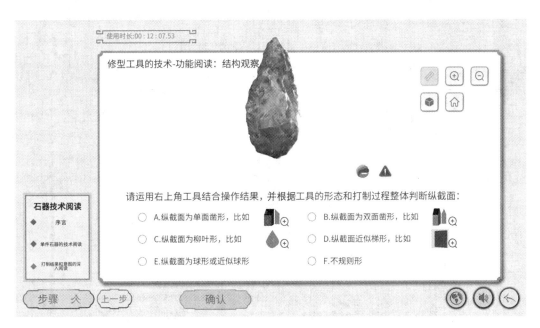

图 1-135 修型工具的纵截面观察之学以致用

(5)修型工具的技术-功能阅读之制作过程复原。

点击"下一步",进入"制作过程复原"。学生通过旋转观察石器模型,经由选择原料、粗制成型、工具生成到最后判断打制过程与方式四步,学习不同的两面器制作过程。本知识点提供两个不同的石器模型,代表两种不同的制作策略(图1-136~图1-143)。

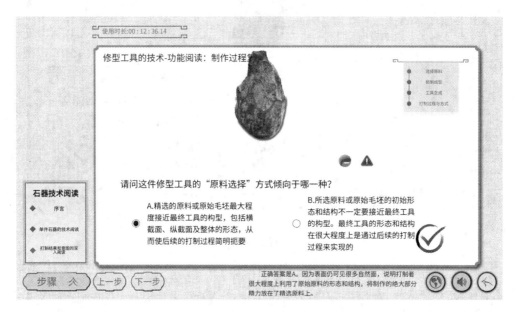

图 1-136  修型工具制作过程的学以致用(1)

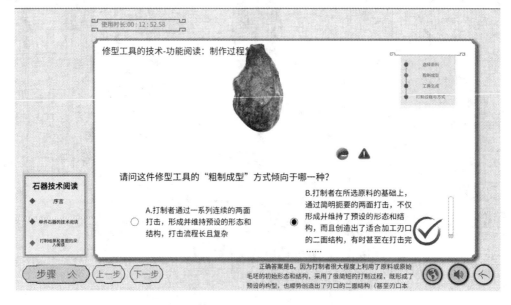

图 1-137  修型工具制作过程的学以致用(2)

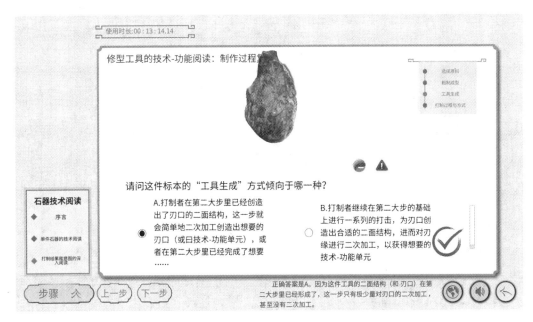

图 1-138　修型工具制作过程的学以致用(3)

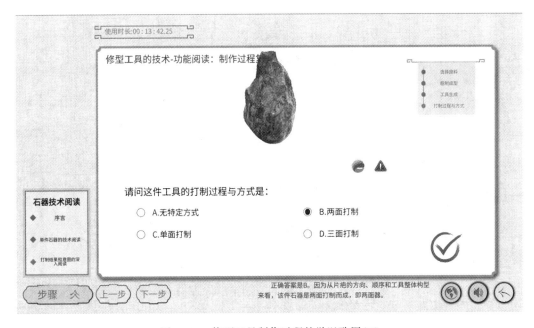

图 1-139　修型工具制作过程的学以致用(4)

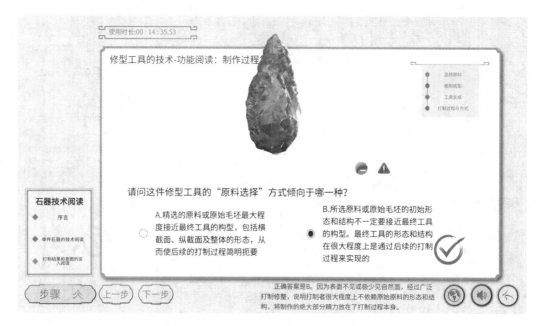

图 1-140 修型工具制作过程的学以致用(5)

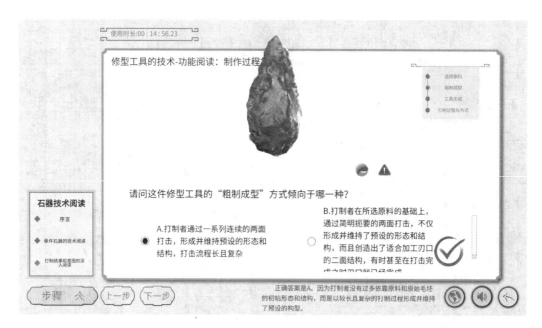

图 1-141 修型工具制作过程的学以致用(6)

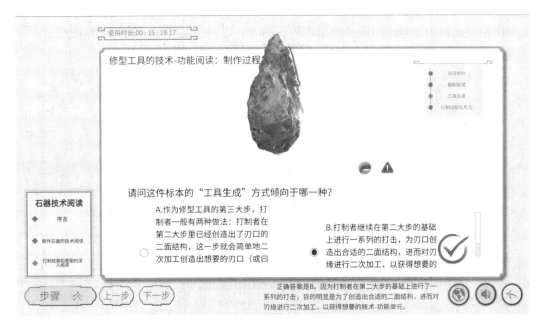

图1-142 修型工具制作过程的学以致用(7)

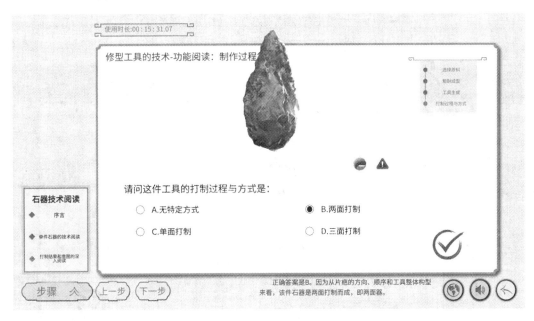

图1-143 修型工具制作过程的学以致用(8)

(6)修型工具的技术-功能阅读之功能单元的区分与展示。

点击"下一步",进入"功能单元的区分与展示",学习相关理论知识。而后点击"下一步"通过旋转和观察标本的 3D 模型，判断该工具的潜在刃口及其不同视角的形态特征。本知识点提供了两个不同刃口形态的石器工具以供学习(图 1-144~图 1-152)。

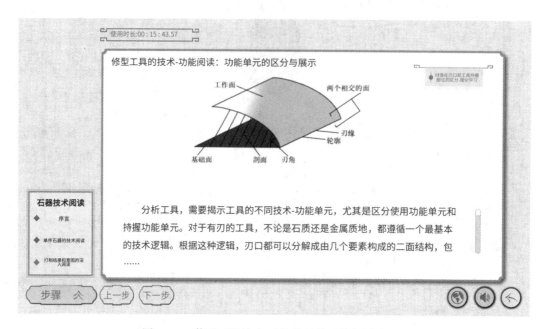

图 1-144　修型工具技术-功能单元的区分与展示(1)

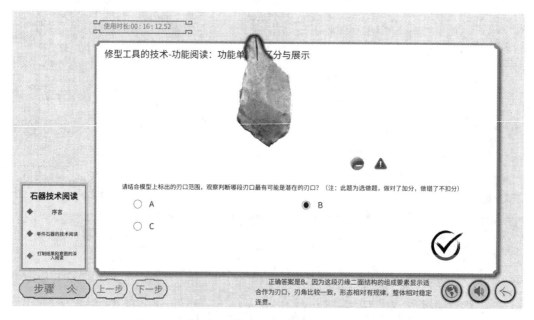

图 1-145　修型工具技术-功能单元的区分与展示(2)

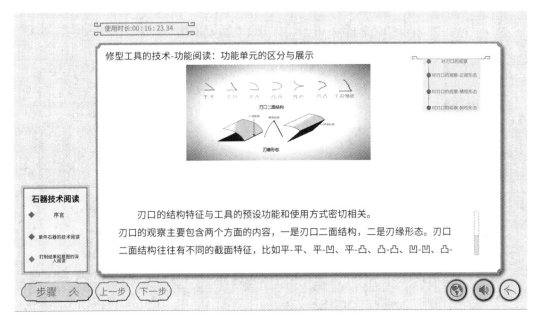

图 1-146 修型工具技术-功能单元的区分与展示(3)

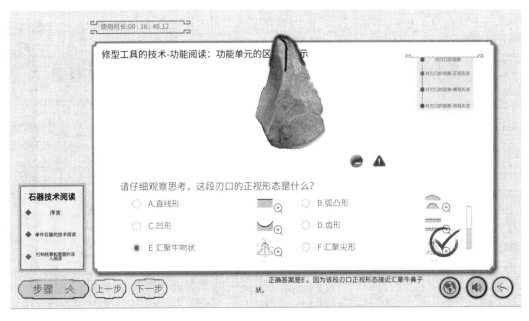

图 1-147 修型工具的技术-功能阅读之刃口正视形态的判断(1)

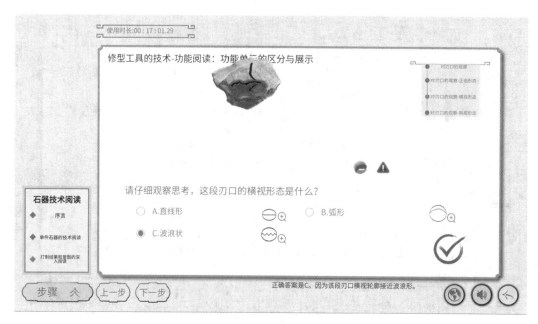

图1-148 修型工具的技术-功能阅读之刃口横视形态的判断(1)

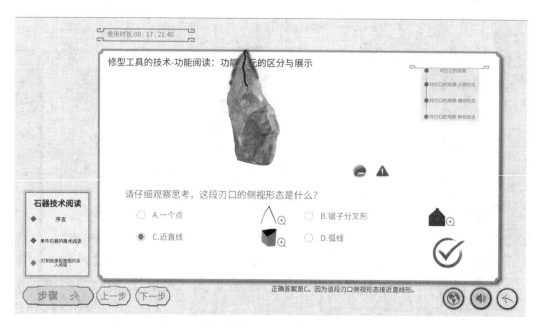

图1-149 修型工具的技术-功能阅读之刃口侧视形态的判断(1)

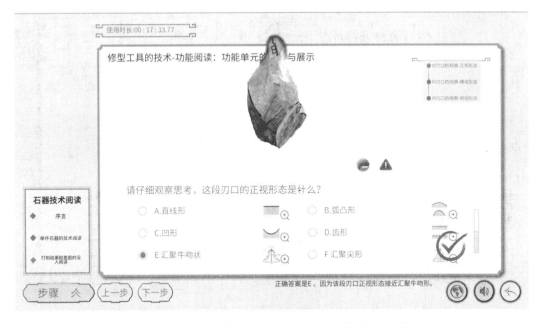

图 1-150 修型工具的技术-功能阅读之刃口正视形态的判断(2)

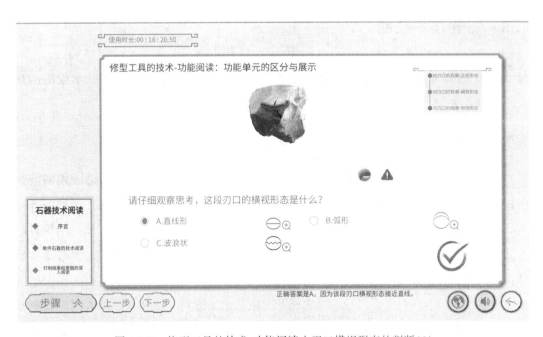

图 1-151 修型工具的技术-功能阅读之刃口横视形态的判断(2)

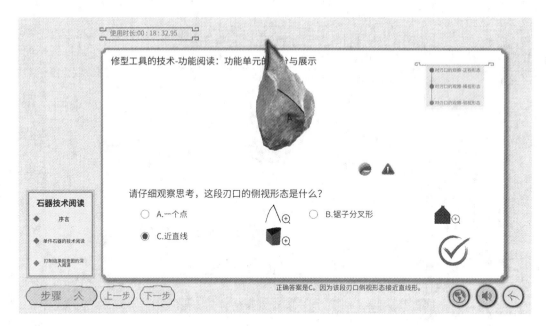

图 1-152　修型工具的技术-功能阅读之刃口侧视形态的判断(2)

## 1.5　石器技术绘图

返回"探索之旅"模块,点击"石器技术绘图",进入序言,了解石器技术绘图的基本原则和方法。

### 1.5.1　序言

石器技术绘图是技术研究者必须掌握的一项技能,它与第三模块的石器技术阅读紧密相关。石器技术绘图包括两种:一是石器传统图,二是石器技术分析图。两种图既有关联,又有区别。二者都必须以石器技术阅读为基础,展现的都是技术阅读的结果。所不同的是,石器传统图旨在展现石器整体表面包括片疤的阴影和立体效果,而石器技术分析图仅保留自然面而不展现片疤同心波和立体效果,同时以多种约定俗成的标识如箭头、数字、字母、颜色等来表现石器表面状况或片疤的方向、顺序和数量,同时表现石器的结构和潜在刃口的技术特征。石器技术分析图是世界旧石器技术研究与交流的通行语言,构成了研究的基石。本模块将展示石片、石核与修型工具的绘制过程,学习绘图的规则和要点(图 1-153)。

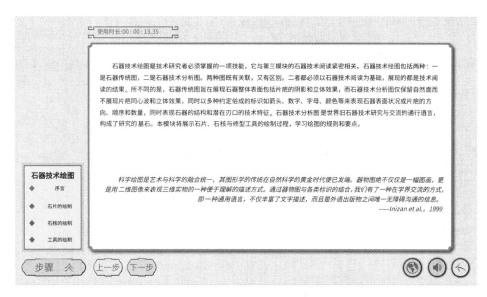

图 1-153　石器技术绘图的意义阐述

## 1.5.2　石片的绘制

石片的绘制

◎ **实验步骤:**

点击"下一步"或侧边标题栏,进入"石片的绘制",通过控制视频进度按钮,观看石片技术绘图的教学视频,回答相关问题。

(1)准备绘图工具。请注意观察视频中出现的绘图工具种类(图 1-154)。

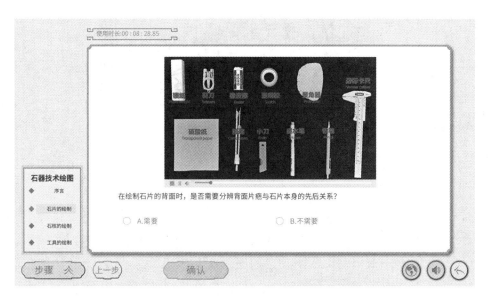

图 1-154　准备绘图工具

（2）根据之前所学知识，正确观察与摆放石片（图1-155）。

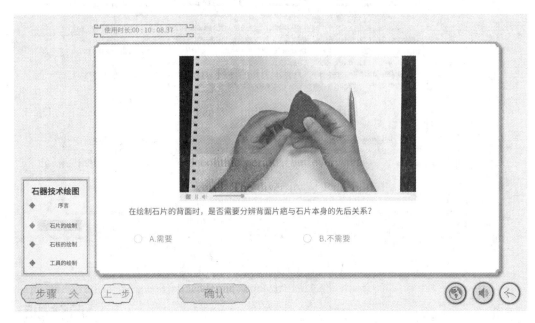

图1-155 观察与摆放石片

（3）摆放好石片之后，开始绘制石片的轮廓（图1-156）。

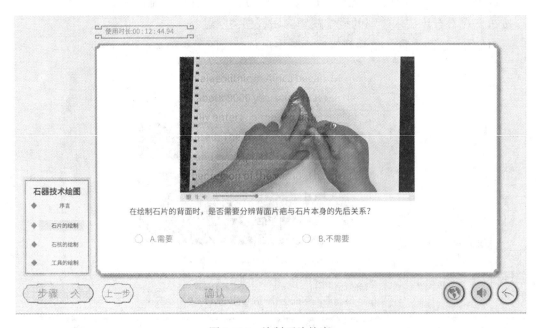

图1-156 绘制石片轮廓

（4）继续绘制石片上的片疤（图1-157）。

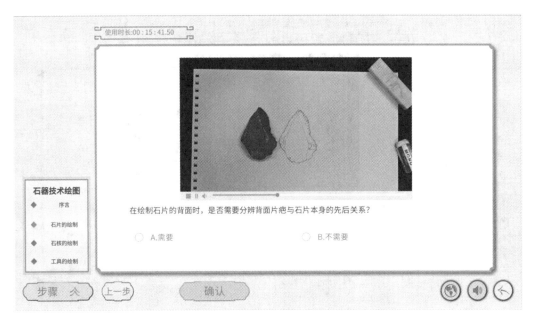

图 1-157 绘制石片片疤

（5）绘制石片的侧面、腹面和台面（图1-158）。

图 1-158 绘制石片侧面、腹面和台面

(6)判断和标注石片背面之前剥片的片疤方向和顺序(图 1-159)。

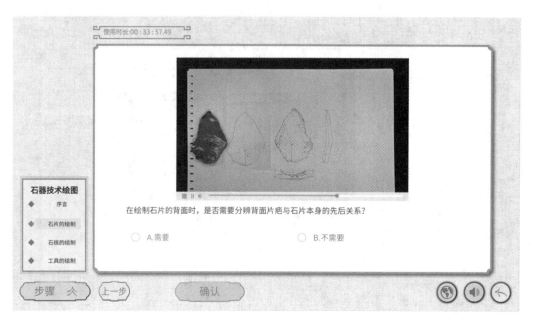

图 1-159 标注片疤方向和顺序

(7)硫酸纸透图并扫描线图(图 1-160)。

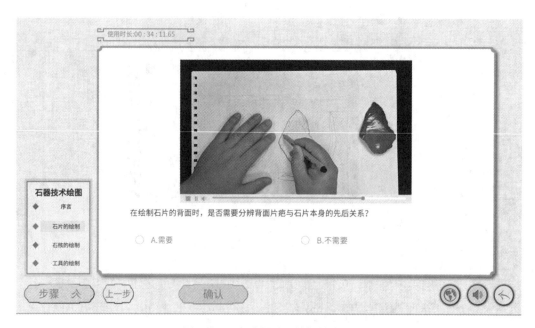

图 1-160 硫酸纸透图并扫描线图

(8)电脑软件处理线图。在保留传统线图的同时,在技术分析图上用箭头标注片疤的打击方向,用数字标注之前片疤的先后顺序,在一旁备注相关技术符号的含义,完成石片的技术分析图。总结相关绘图要点,回答相关测试问题(图1-161~图1-162)。

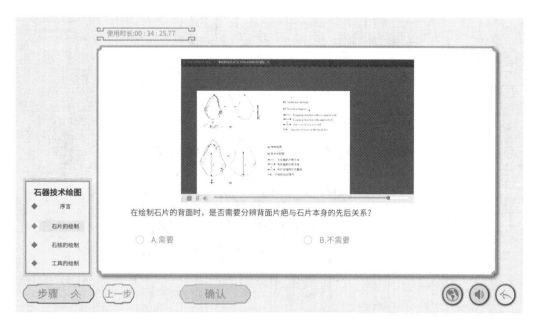

图 1-161　电脑软件处理线图

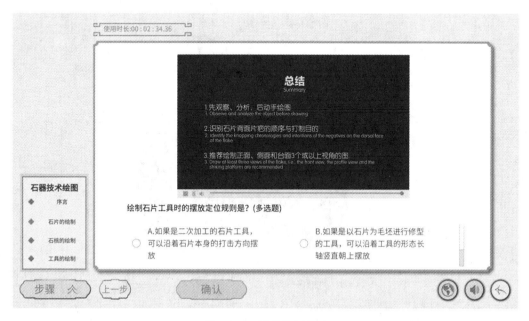

图 1-162　石片绘制总结

### 1.5.3 石核的绘制

石核的绘制

◎ **实验步骤：**

点击"下一步"或侧边标题栏，进入"石核的绘制"，通过控制视频进度按钮观看石核技术绘图的教学视频，回答相关问题。

（1）准备绘图工具（图 1-163）。

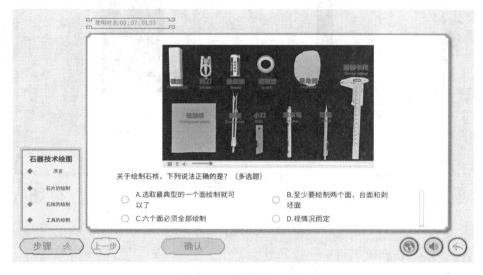

图 1-163 准备绘图工具

（2）根据之前所学知识，正确观察与摆放石核（图 1-164）。

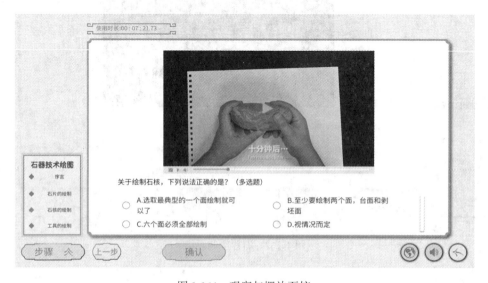

图 1-164 观察与摆放石核

（3）依次绘制石核的轮廓、剥坯面、台面并标注剥片顺序（图1-165）。

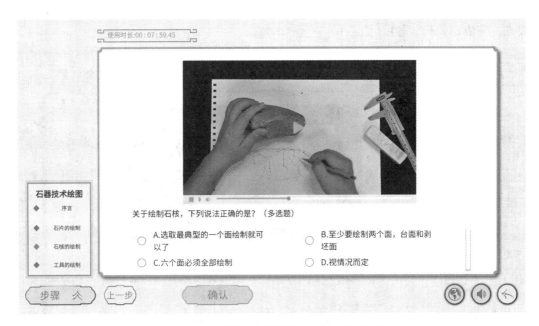

图1-165 绘制石核的轮廓、剥坯面和台面

（4）完成初步绘制后，继续使用硫酸纸透图并扫描（图1-166）。

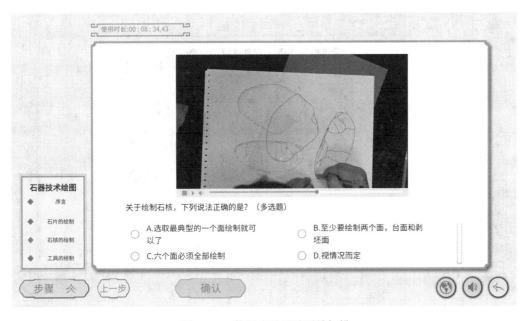

图1-166 使用硫酸纸透图并扫描

（5）电脑软件处理线图，根据石核的技术特征，展示其剥坯的过程，包括每个片疤的作用和目的，剥坯顺序和方向等，在一旁备注技术符号的含义。最后总结石核绘图的要点，完成相关测试题目（图 1-167~图 1-168）。

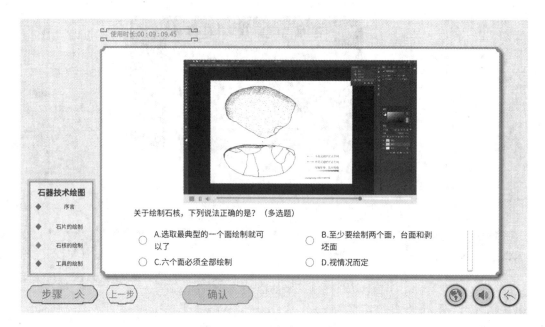

图 1-167　电脑软件处理线图

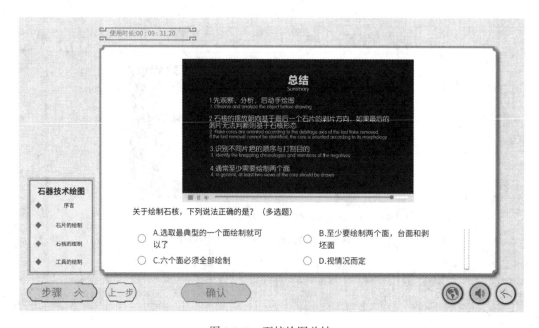

图 1-168　石核绘图总结

## 1.5.4　工具的绘制

工具的绘制

### ◎ 实验步骤：

点击"下一步"或侧边标题栏，进入"工具的绘制"，通过控制视频进度按钮观看工具技术绘图的教学视频，回答相关问题。

(1)准备绘图工具(图 1-169)。

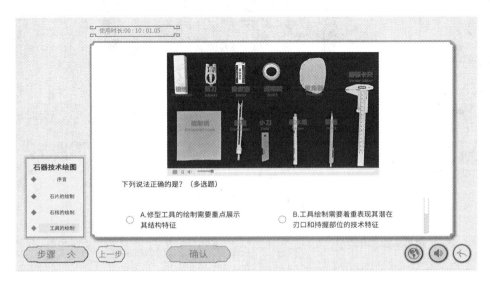

图 1-169　准备绘图工具

(2)根据之前学习的知识，正确观察与摆放工具(图 1-170)。

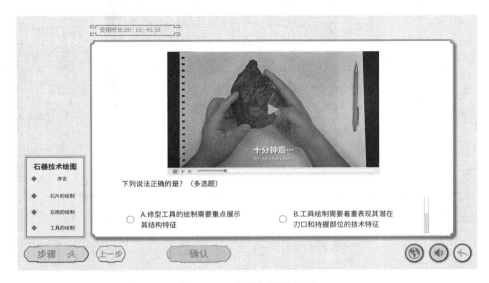

图 1-170　观察与摆放工具

（3）该标本为两面器，绘制两面轮廓和片疤等（图 1-171）。

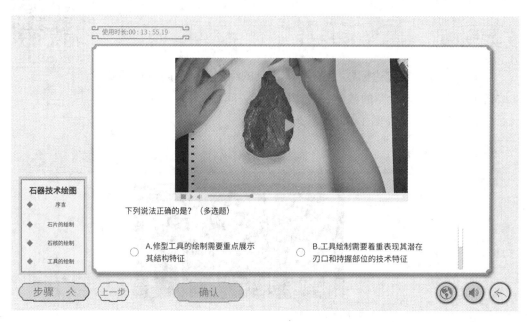

图 1-171　绘制两面轮廓和片疤

（4）绘制侧面（图 1-172）。

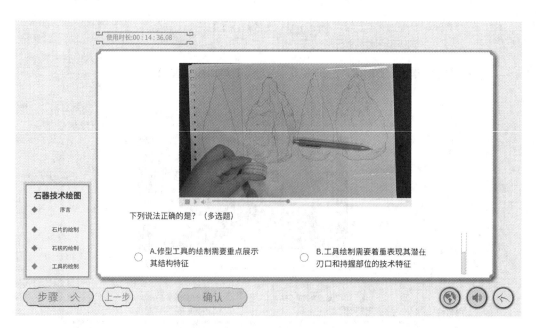

图 1-172　绘制两面器的侧面

(5)绘制横截面(图1-173)。

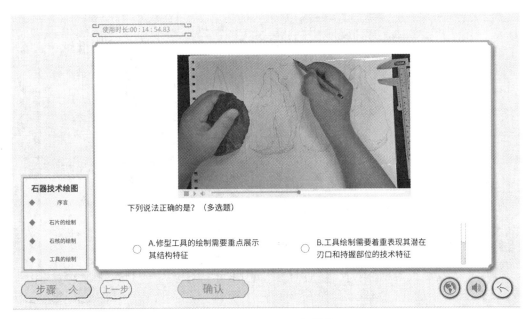

图1-173 绘制两面器的横截面

(6)根据之前学到的知识,区分该工具的使用-功能单元和持握-功能单元(图1-174)。

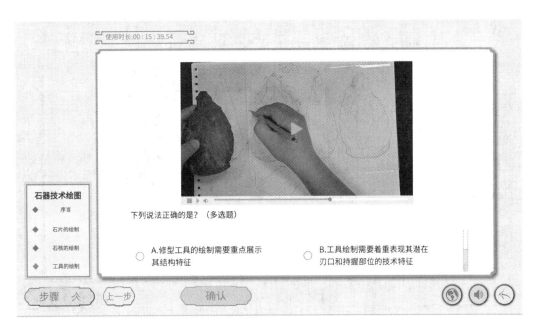

图1-174 区分使用-功能单元和持握-功能单元并标注相关技术特征

（7）硫酸纸透图并扫描（图 1-175）。

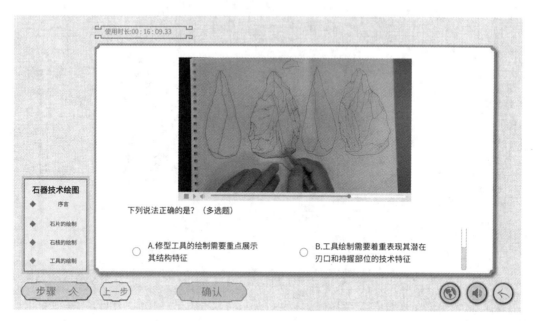

图 1-175　硫酸纸透图并扫描

（8）电脑软件处理线图。完成技术-生产分析图和技术-功能分析图，并在一旁备注技术符号的含义。总结该工具绘图的要点并回答问题(图 1-176～图 1-177)。

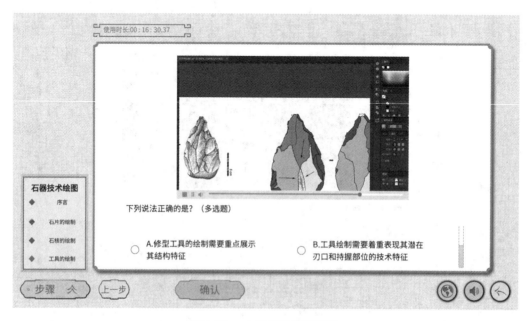

图 1-176　电脑软件处理线图

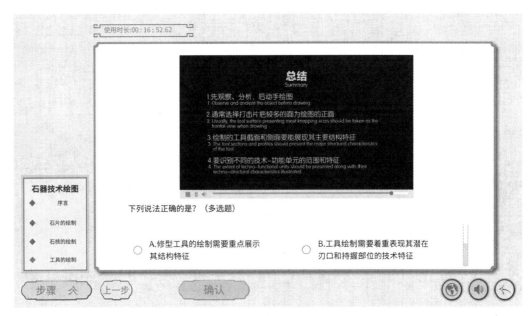

图 1-177 工具绘制总结

# 第2章 考核之路

## 2.1 理论考核

◎ 实验步骤：

点击"考核之路"，进入世界旧石器技术考核之路。考核之路分为三个模块：理论考核、石器技术阅读考核、石器拼合实验考核。三个考核模块可以任意顺序进行考核，但所有考核必须全部完成后，才算完成"考核之路"。完成考核后，系统将显示一个得分页面，该分数计入最后考核得分(图2-1)。

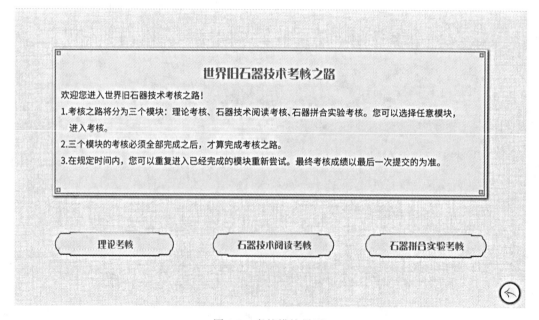

图2-1 考核模块界面

点击进入"考核之路"模块后，进行理论考核，依次点击下一步直至做完所有选择题(图2-2)。

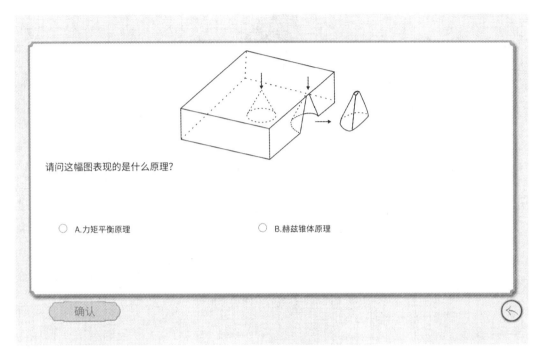

请问这幅图表现的是什么原理?

○ A.力矩平衡原理　　　　　　　　　　○ B.赫兹锥体原理

确认

图2-2　赫兹锥体理论考核

## 2.2　石器技术阅读考核

◎ 实验步骤:

点击进入"考核之路"模块后，进行石器技术阅读考核，观察系统随机发放的石器模型并回答所有问题(图2-3)。

## 2.3　石器拼合实验考核

◎ 实验步骤:

点击进入"考核之路"模块后，进行石器拼合实验考核，观察全部石器并根据提示完成拼合(图2-4)。

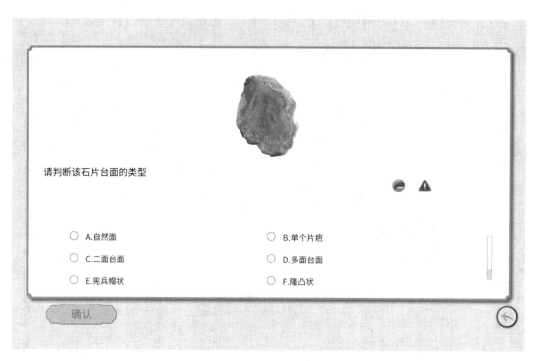

请判断该石片台面的类型

○ A.自然面          ○ B.单个片疤

○ C.二面台面        ○ D.多面台面

○ E.宪兵帽状        ○ F.隆凸状

确认

图 2-3　石器技术阅读考核

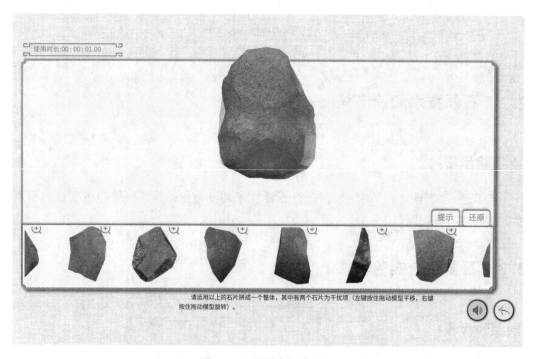

使用时长:00:00:01.00

提示　还原

请运用以上的石片拼成一个整体,其中有两个石片为干扰项(左键按住拖动模型平移,右键
按住拖动模型旋转)。

图 2-4　石器拼合实验考核

# 第3章 实验平台操作与技术说明

## 3.1 登录虚拟仿真实验平台的操作说明

(1)校内人员：使用学生账号和密码进入武汉大学虚拟仿真平台。

(2)校外人员：通过实名认证后进入实验平台。

(3)进入实验平台后，可以看到"实验原理""探索之旅""考核之路""参考资料""实验成绩"等模块，点开即可看到相应的内容。

(4)完成"考核之路"模块后，点击实验成绩，可查看并上传学生本人成绩。

## 3.2 使用平台时特殊的技术操作说明

(1)单击任意模块开始探索，不必从头到尾依次学习。

(2)点击标本图片或3D模型旁边的 ⚠ 符号，可以获取该标本的来源、年代等信息。

(3)所有石器标本3D模型的旋转方法：按住鼠标右键抓取3D模型，即可旋转标本。

(4)所有石器标本3D模型均有高清链接，请点击 ⬤ 这个图标查看该标本的"云端地球"高清3D模型。

(5)每个模块的学习进度无法在网络上保存，请一次性完成每个模块的学习。

## 3.3 "云端地球"超链接说明

(1)点击圆形"云端地球"图案 ⬤ ，跳转至对应标本的"云端地球"链接。

　　(2)按住鼠标左键或右键可以拖动、旋转标本,从不同视角观察标本;也可以通过鼠标滚轮来实现放大和缩小 3D 模型,以便观察标本细节(图 3-1)。

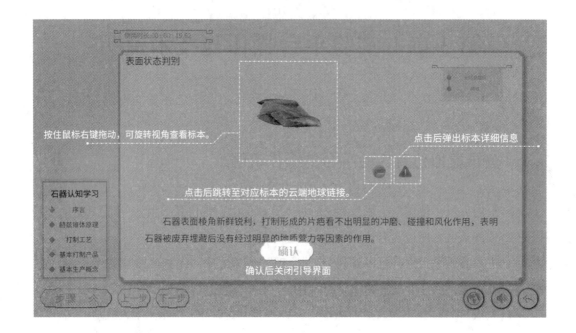

图 3-1　鼠标操作说明

## 3.4　其他说明

　　(1)界面左侧是步骤菜单和进度指示条,小步骤可以任意跳转。

　　(2)正在进行中的步骤显示为橙色,已完成或未完成步骤为灰色。

　　(3)进入探索之旅后,每完成一个模块的学习,会在"探索之旅"界面显示已完成。

# 术语解释汇总

**赫兹锥体原理**：赫兹锥体是物体穿过固体时产生的锥体，如子弹穿过玻璃。严格地说，它是一种从撞击点穿过具有脆性、非晶态或隐晶态固体材料时形成的力的锥体。这个力最终在原料上留下一个完整或不完整的锥体。这种物理原理可以解释石制品制作过程中石片的形态和特征。

**打制工艺**：工艺一般是指剥离下石片所采用的施力、打制手段以及动作姿势，通常包括锤击、碰砧、砸击和压制等工艺。工艺属于打制石器技术系统知识的初级层次。

**锤击法**：锤击是运用石锤，集中力量，借助赫兹锥体原理，打击石料表面靠近边缘的某一点，将石料剥裂开的一种工艺与过程，既可用来产生石片毛坯，也可以用来加工工具。根据石锤与原料之间有无中介的存在，锤击又可分为直接锤击和间接锤击。

**碰砧法**：碰砧是用手持石料，向另一石块即石砧上碰击以便剥裂石片的工艺与过程。

**砸击法**：砸击是将石料垫在石砧上，用石锤以合适的角度和力度砸石料，以分裂石料的工艺与过程。

**摔碰法**：摔碰是采用站立的姿势，将手中的石料摔投到石砧上，从而使原料碎裂的一种工艺。

**压制法**：压制是用一个很尖的工具压石块或石片、石叶的边缘使之更加规整的工艺，可以用来加工工具，也可以剥离细石叶。

**砾石**：砾石是远古人类在河滩拣选的用于打制石器的原料，通常是经过流水搬运冲磨和风化后形成的表面光滑无尖锐棱角的天然岩石，也称为河卵石。因搬运距离和水流动能不同，河卵石表面磨圆度有差异。河滩上的砾石通常都被搬运远离其原生矿脉，属于次生埋藏。地质学上根据尺寸又将其分为细砾、粗砾和巨砾。旧石器考古中一般以 7 厘米为界（也有以 10 厘米为界）将砾石分为大型砾石（Cobble）和小型砾石（Pebble），超过 25 厘米者为巨型砾石（Boulder）。

**矿脉结核**：矿脉结核是远古人类在山区岩矿条带堆积处开采的用于打制石器的原

料，地质学上是指在成分、结构、颜色等方面与围岩有显著区别，且与围岩间有明显界面的矿物集合体。它们往往发育在山脉岩层中，古人开采的通常是这些矿物集合体里面经风化或因其他原因暴露、剥落下来的质地相对均匀、各向同性的岩块或结核，未经过水或风力等的搬运，属于原生埋藏。

**灰岩角砾：** 石灰岩洞穴或岩厦中常有因风化等原因剥落下来的块状岩石，主要矿物成分有碳酸盐、方解石，硬度较燧石等略低，因风化或水作用程度不同表面棱角尖锐程度有差异，有些表面还有钙质结核附着。远古人类常从中拣选合适的石块用于打制石器的原料。

**石片：** 石片是从石质母体上剥离下的产品，剩下的母体一般称为石核。由于赫兹锥体原理的作用，石片具有相似的可以辨认的特征，包括台面、打击点、打击泡、同心波、背面、腹面、石片角、打击方向、放射线。

**石核：** 考古遗址中所见的石核一般是剥坯完成后剩下的石块。由于赫兹锥体原理的作用，石核表面会产生可以辨认的一些特征，包括台面、打击点、反泡、纵脊、台面角、剥坯面、打击方向、放射线、同心波等。理论上石核与石片本属于同一个母体石块，二者的区别在于，石片台面下方一般会有一个突出的打击泡，而石核上对应的位置是一个凹陷，即反泡。

**生产概念：** 生产概念是指打制者获得毛坯或工具的方式。从理论上看，世界旧石器技术演化中主要有两种宏观的生产概念，即剥坯和修型。

**剥坯：** 剥坯是指运用多种工艺将石料剥裂成不同形态和大小的毛坯的过程，所获毛坯既可直接使用，也可根据需要修整成工具。从技术上看，剥坯的目的是从石核上获得毛坯，结果将产生两类产品：剥坯后的石核和石片，而且石核与石片在操作链中具有不同的地位和作用。想要从石料上打下所需的石片毛坯，打制者有两种方式：第一种是通过选择合适形态结构的石料，直接从上面打击剥离下想要的石片，未对石核进行人工准备。第二种需要对石料进行一定程度的预制，比如台面和剥坯面的准备，然后从准备好的石核上打下目标石片。在剥坯的生产体系中，打制者的目的是获得石片作为工具毛坯，或者直接使用，或者二次加工成特定刃口。

**剥坯面：** 剥坯面指石核上产生预设的目标石片的那个面，它与台面是相交的，交角小于90°。剥坯面具有一定的技术特征，比如远端和两侧要有一定的弧凸度。

**修型：** 修型是指按照预设产品的形态和技术特征，对一块合适的石坯从一开始就进行循序渐进的打制，直到将其制作成所需要的形制和大小。修型反映的是从坯料到成品的连续递减过程。简单地说，修型打下来的石片是打制者不需要的，这与剥坯的目的相反。修型类似于雕塑的过程。

拼合分析：它是通过将不同的石制品根据"表面接合"和/或"厚度接合"的方式拼接在一起，从而理解石器打制的先后顺序和过程。它是旧石器考古的重要研究方法之一，早在19世纪末就被应用。20世纪60年代，随着田野发掘记录方法的改进和"操作链"等研究理念的兴起，学者们开始在石器分析中较为频繁地使用该方法。

技术阅读：为了确定每件石制品在操作链中的确切位置，必须首先"阅读"石器表面打击片疤的方向，排列出它们的先后顺序，然后整合所有材料判断石器在整个石器工业中的地位。对于单件石制品，必须对其打制过程和每个打制动作所产生的结果进行阅读分析。阅读石器可以让我们了解打制者使用的原料、技术动作和背后的知识，这些因素最终导致工具的生成。

技术-功能单元：基于"以刃口为先"的理论，"技术-功能单元"被定义为"一组通过协同作用整合在一起的技术要素和(或)技术特征"，一个工具必须由至少两个技术-功能单元构成，一个是使用-功能单元，另一个是持握-功能单元。

石器技术分析图：石器传统图旨在展现石器整体表面，包括片疤的阴影和立体效果。而石器技术分析图仅保留自然面而不展现片疤同心波和立体效果，同时以多种约定俗成的标识如箭头、数字、字母、颜色等来表现石器表面状况或片疤的方向、顺序和数量，同时表现石器的结构和潜在刃口的技术特征。石器技术分析图是世界旧石器技术研究与交流的通行语言，构成了研究的基石。

# World Paleolithic Technology Virtual Simulation Experiment: A Practical Coursebook

# Preface

The development of virtual simulation courses and various types of MOOC courses over the last decade has made it possible to relieve knowledge teaching from any location confinement, as well as to establish a nationwide and international course on Palaeolithic technology. Since the study of Paleolithic technology requires frequent use of stone specimens from all over the world and precise three-dimensional display and observation of stone specimens, virtual simulation technology can be a powerful assistant for this course. Thus, a course on World Paleolithic Technology was constructed using virtual simulation.

Since the 1960s, technological research under the concept of "*chaîne opératoire*" has gradually become the mainstream method and goal of Palaeolithic research worldwide. This trend of Paleolithic research, originated from France, has formed a distinctive technological theory and methodology system after nearly 30 years of development. In the 1990s, with the opening up and increase of academic exchanges between China and foreign countries, French theories and methods about Paleolithic research were introduced into Chinese Paleolithic archaeological academia, which brought new ideas of research and pushed forward the internationalization of Paleolithic research in China. In the last 20 years, under the direct influence of French scholars, technological research has gradually become the main method of Chinese Paleolithic research and has been continuously applied to practice. This has produced a large number of achievements while causing doubts about it and errors in practice, partly because of a lack of systematic training and comprehensive understanding of Paleolithic technology. Currently, there has been no general course on Paleolithic technology in China, and students learn the knowledge about it mostly from teachers or by themselves. This situation also leads to the fact that the understanding of related concepts varies from person to person, and it is difficult for different researchers to have academic exchanges at the same level. Thus, there is an urgent need for a systematic course on Palaeolithic technology that should be accessible to as many students as possible.

This coursebook is mainly composed of two core parts: knowledge learning and assessment learning. Knowledge learning mainly introduces the relevant concepts and terms of technological studies, the basic concepts and products of knapping, the knapping process, the refitting experiments, the technical description, the technical drawing, and so on. Assessment learning, mainly represented in the form of questions, is used to examine the effectiveness of knowledge learning while consolidating the old knowledge. In addition, the coursebook also provides relevant references and summarizes the core bibliographies on Palaeolithic research so that students can easily access and study in depth relevant information after class. This course is a part of the undergraduate courses *Culture and Technology of Ancient Humans*, *Archaeology and Human Civilization Process*, *World Paleolithic Archaeology* and the postgraduate courses *Paleolithic Archaeology* and *Stone Tool Identification and Research*. In this coursebook, each module is arranged in a particular order, which is not necessarily followed during learning.

"Paleolithic technology" represents a research method that needs to combine theory and practice and should be practiced constantly. It is a field that needs to be openly exchanged and mutually discussed among different researchers and a system that needs to be deeply and prudently considered during the final interpretation of "seeing humans through the artifacts". It's only in this way can we really touch the logic and law of stone tool technology and "see humans through the stone tools". It is hoped that this virtual simulation course can contribute to the establishment of a relatively unified system for the study of Paleolithic technology, and more importantly, inspire the readers to take the initiative to use technological thinking in the future study of stone artifacts.

The software development of the corresponding course on "World Paleolithic Technology Virtual Simulation Experiment" has been funded by Archaeological Institute for Yangtze Civilization, and Lab & Equipment Administration Department of Wuhan University. The lithic artifacts used for 3D modeling, in addition to our own collection, were mainly collected from University of Paris X-Nanterre, France, with the permission of Prof. Eric Boëda and from Institut de Paléontologie Humaine, France, with the permission of Prof. Henry de Lumley. Associate Researcher Stéphanie Bonilauri of the Muséum National d'Histoire Naturelle, France provided us many helps during the collection. The collection and 3D modeling of some lithic specimens were also supported by colleagues from Hubei Provincial

Institute of Cultural Relics and Archaeology, Yunnan Provincial Institute of Cultural Relics and Archaeology, Guangxi Institute of Cultural Relics Protection and Archeology, Hunan Provincial Institute of Cultural Relics and Archaeology, and Chongqing China Three Gorges Museum, *etc*. In addition to our team's graduate students who are authors of this coursebook, the construction of the three-dimensional models of stone tools was significantly assisted by Sunbin Huang, a PhD student, and Marie-Josée Angue Zogo, a postgraduate student, from Muséum National d'Histoire Naturelle, France. The software and platform for the 3D modeling were provided and supported by Wuhan Daspatial Technology Co., Ltd. The professors and colleagues from Institute of Vertebrate Paleontology and Paleoanthropology of Chinese Academy of Sciences, Beijing University, Jilin University, Shandong University, Zhejiang University, Hebei Normal University, Minzu University of China, Hubei University, South-Central Minzu University, Shanxi University, as well as the School of History and the School of Law of Wuhan University, *etc*., either discussed and exchanged views with the editor-in-chief of this coursebook, or provided professional guidance and support in 3D modeling, teaching practice, and first-class course application. Several colleagues from the Department of Archaeology helped a lot in maintaining the experiment software, implementing the project, applying for software copyrights. In the several assessments organized by Wuhan University, the experts put forward a lot of constructive comments, which pushed the software and the course to improve continuously. The deepest gratitude should be given to all of them.

Finally, due to the author's ability and time constraints, errors are inevitable in the virtual simulation experimental software and coursebook, so please do not hesitate to correct them.

**Authors**

February 1,2024

# Table of Contents

# Introduction

Stone tools, usually with cutting edges, were frequently used by the ancient people in their daily life to cut, chop, scrap, dig, drill, etc. Because the relatively regular morphology and structure, stone tools dating from the Late Paleolithic period to the Neolithic period are relatively easy to identify and analyze (e.g., arrowheads, axes, adzes, chisels, etc.). However, as the morphology of stone tools dating from the Early and Mid-Paleolithic periods is extremely irregular, it is difficult to reveal in depth the concepts and methods of the makers based on the morphology alone. Guided by the research theories about Paleolithic technology, this course takes the stone products excavated from archaeological sites as the research objects, and reconstructs the "*chaîne opératoire*" of stone tools from raw material selection to blank production and instrumentalisation in a dynamic and integrated way. It aims at revealing and understanding the intention and cognition of the maker, as well as exploring the commonalities and differences between Paleolithic technology and the ancient techno-cultures around the world.

## ◎ Experimental Steps:

Log into the virtual simulation experimental teaching project management platform of Wuhan University to view this project ( https://xfsy. whu. edu. cn/website/resources/list. action), or visit the website directly ( http://210. 42. 121. 113/ShiQi/) and enter the homepage of *World Paleolithic Technology Virtual Simulation Experiment*; click on the "Experimental Principles" button, and enter the "Experimental Principles" section ( Figure 0-1 ). Understanding the importance of stone tools and the study of lithic technology is important for us to recover the process of stone tool making, explain the intention of the maker, and explore the evolution of lithic technology and the diversity of ancient techno-cultures worldwide.

Experimental principles

Stone tools were used by hominins in their daily life. Most of them had an active working edge for cutting, chopping, scraping and drilling, etc. The stone tools of upper Palaeolithic and Neolithic periods are relatively easy for recognizing their nature and function via comparison and analogy because they usually have standardized morphology and structure (e.g., arrow, axe, adze, chisel). In contrast, the stone tools of Lower and middle Palaeolithic are often not regular in morphology, and thus difficult for revealing the intentions of their makers. Guided by theories of Palaeolithic technology, this virtual simulation course uses stone artifacts excavated from...

*Making silent stones speak: Human evolution and the dawn of technology.*
—*Kathy D. Schick & Nicholas Toth*, 1993

Figure 0-1    Experimental Principles Interface

# Chapter 1   Journey of Exploration

## ◎ Experimental Steps：

Return to the homepage of "World Paleolithic Technology Virtual Simulation Experiment", and click on the "Journey of Exploration" button to pop up a map of the world (Figure 1-1). Click on Africa, Europe, Asia, America, and Oceania on the map in turn, and the system will pop up their respective Paleolithic culture overview.

Figure 1-1   World Map of the Start Exploring Screen

# 1.1    Overview of Paleolithic Cultures of the World

## 1.1.1    Overview of African Paleolithic Cultures

The Palaeolithic in Africa began 3.3 million years ago. It was not until about 9,000 years ago that the Neolithic period began, although different sub-regions were not synchronised. The continent has the longest Palaeolithic period, but every phase of the Palaeolithic predates almost every other region of the world. The diversity of Palaeolithic technology and culture in Africa goes far beyond Clark's linear generalisation expressed as "Mode I-V". The developmental sequence of the Palaeolithic culture in Africa was defined differently from that in Europe: Earlier Stone Age, Middle Stone Age and Later Stone Age. These terms themselves reflect a specific academic context and are inextricably linked to the local characteristics of the Palaeolithic technology in the region. The African Palaeolithic culture has a wide spatial and temporal presence and is rich in technological facies (Figure 1-2).

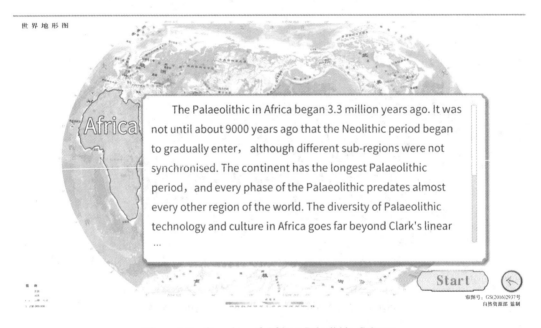

Figure 1-2    Overview of African Paleolithic Cultures

## 1.1.2  Overview of European Paleolithic Cultures

The first Europeans appeared between 1.5 and 1.2 million years ago, and the European Palaeolithic culture lasted until about 11,000 years ago, with some regional discrepancies. The relatively clear evolution of Palaeolithic cultures in Western and Southern Europe goes through different stages: Pre-Acheulian—Acheulian—Mousterian—Chatelperronian—Aurignacian—Gravettian—Solutrean—Magdalenian. As Central and Eastern Europe witness more significant regional differences in the Palaeolithic culture than Western and Southern Europe, it is not possible to generalize their Palaeolithic culture with the technological history of Western and Southern Europe. Generally speaking, the European Palaeolithic culture has a wide spatial and temporal distribution and is rich in technological facies (Figure 1-3).

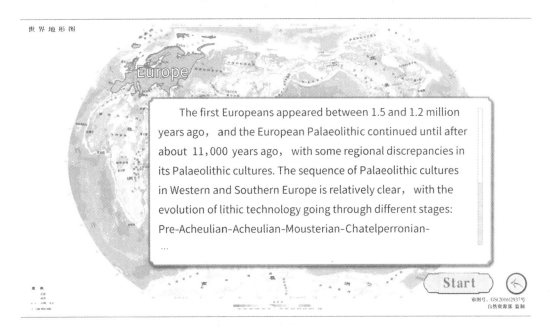

Figure 1-3   Overview of European Paleolithic Cultures

## 1.1.3  Overview of Asian Paleolithic Cultures

The Palaeolithic in Asia began at least over 2.5 million years ago and lasted until around 10,000 years ago. The Palaeolithic technology in Asia was regionally diverse; except South and West Asia, the Central, North, East and Southeast Asia as a whole experienced an evolutionary trajectory of lithic technology that differed from that of the Mediterranean and its environs (Western Europe and Africa), with only a few regions or sites yielding technological products similar to those of the Mediterranean world as a result of cultural exchange or technological convergence. The lithic technology in East Asia was characterized by stable and long-lasting successions and presented both cultural exchanges with the West and indigenous innovations. Clear technological changes did not happen until the Late Palaeolithic that began ca. 50,000-40,000 years ago. The Asian Palaeolithic as a whole has a wide spatial and temporal distribution with abundant technological histories (Figure 1-4).

Figure 1-4    Overview of Asian Paleolithic Cultures

## 1.1.4    Overview of American Paleolithic Cultures

The Palaeolithic in the Americas began at least 40,000 years ago, with a considerable number of sites dating from 20,000-15,000 years ago. It was not until around 10,000 years ago that the continent entered the Archaic or Paleoindian period (the Late Palaeolithic in the Americas), and saw the end of the Palaeolithic spanning from 7,000 to around 3,000 years ago with an uneven spatial distribution. Traditionally, the earliest American culture was thought to be the Clovis Culture (which began 13,500 years ago), the existence of which caused controversy among scholars because of archaeological discoveries and research in the past 20 years. The Pre-Clovis Culture is not a unified cultural entity, but rather consists of a series of sites which are older than about 14,000 years and of which the technology and industry are different from that of the Clovis Culture. Currently, the earliest archaeological site in North America was dated to ca. 130,000 years ago (a subject of much debates), while more than 100 archaeological levels with stratigraphical context have been found in Central and South America with a dating range of 10,000−50,000 years ago. This indicates that the beginnings of human history in the Americas were much earlier than previously recognized, and that their evolutionary trajectories and technological facies were significantly different from those of the Old World (Figure 1-5).

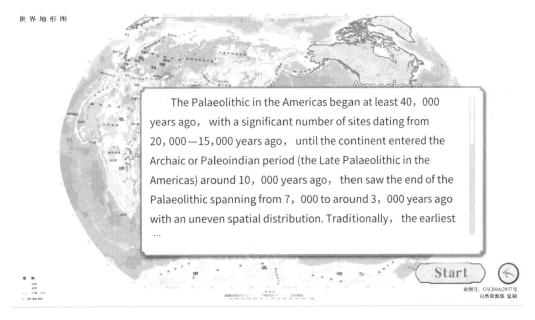

The Palaeolithic in the Americas began at least 40,000 years ago, with a significant number of sites dating from 20,000−15,000 years ago, until the continent entered the Archaic or Paleoindian period (the Late Palaeolithic in the Americas) around 10,000 years ago, then saw the end of the Palaeolithic spanning from 7,000 to around 3,000 years ago with an uneven spatial distribution. Traditionally, the earliest ...

Figure 1-5　Overview of American Paleolithic Cultures

## 1.1.5　Overview of Paleolithic Cultures in Oceania

The earliest human habitation in Oceania dated back to 65,000 years ago, as indicated by the Madjedbebe Rock Shelter site in Kakadu National Park in northern Australia, which suggested that humans may have arrived here around 65,000 years ago across the sea up to 80-100 kilometers wide. The lithic assemblage from this site included grinding stones, fragmented ochres, edge-polished axes, flake tools, pointed tools that might have been used as spear heads and tools for processing food. Of these, the ground stone tools are the earliest in the world, dating to 50,000 years ago. The site contained many ochre blocks and tools for processing ochre. After 50,000 years ago, the number of sites in the Oceania region increased and was not restricted to Australia. Findings from surrounding islands such as eight highland sites in eastern New Guinea confirmed that humans made and used stone tools to exploit plant and animal resources 49,000 − 44,000 years ago, as suggested by knapped stone tools including cobble-based cores, flakes and stone axes. Axe-adze-like objects with polished edge or body dating between 10,000 and 8,000 years ago were found in the eastern highlands of New Guinea, and a flake-tool industry has been found in the islands to the east about 8,000 years ago. In contrast, the earliest humans on the large islands to the east and north of Melanesia were Austronesians, with different technological and cultural traditions. Thus, due to differences in island and marine environments, the overall Palaeolithic history of Oceania was regionally diverse and difficult to compare with the Palaeolithic of the Old World. Some knapped stone tools appeared still in some regions until the arrival of European colonists (Figure 1-6).

Figure 1-6   Overview of Paleolithic Cultures in Oceania

## 1.2　Theoretical Study of Lithic Artifacts

◎ **Experimental Steps:**

After clicking "Start", enter the module "Theoretical Study of Lithic Artifacts" to learn basic knowledge of stone artifacts (Figure 1-7).

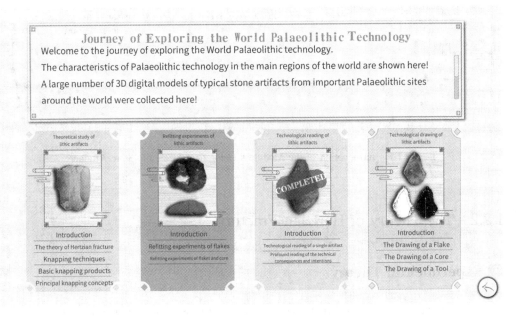

Figure 1-7　Interface of the Journey of Exploring the World Paleolithic Technology

### 1.2.1　Introduction

This part introduces the fundamental knowledge for conducting lithic technological analysis. In this module, you will study the theory of Hertzian fracture, the basic knapping techniques and products, and principal knapping concepts in the lithic production (Figure 1-8).

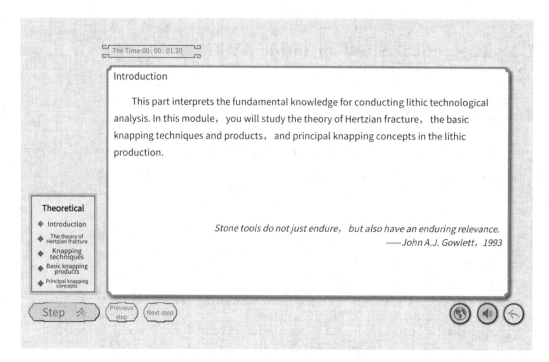

Figure 1-8    Introduction of the Module "Theoretical Study of Lithic Artefacts"

## 1.2.2    The Theory of Hertzian Fracture

◎ **Experimental Theory:**

A Hertzian cone is a cone created when an object passes through a solid, such as a bullet through glass. Strictly speaking, it is a cone of force formed when an object passes through a brittle, amorphous or cryptocrystalline solid material from the point of impact. This force eventually creates a complete or incomplete cone in the raw material. This physical principle explains the morphology and characteristics of flakes during lithic production.

◎ **Experimental Steps:**

Click "Next step" to study the Hertzian cone principles, followed by a multiple-choice question for students to check their understanding about this knowledge; after the students complete the question, analysis of the correct answer will be displayed (Figure 1-9).

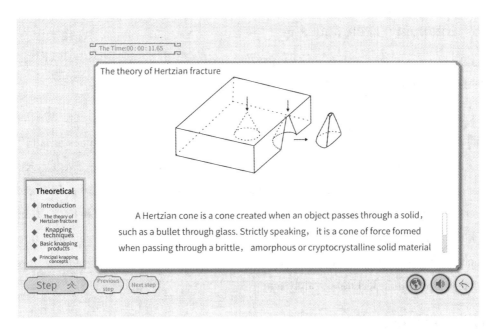

Figure 1-9    Diagrammatic Representation and Explanation of the Hertzian Fracture

Click "Next step", and a choice question waiting for an answer will be displayed (Figure 1-10).

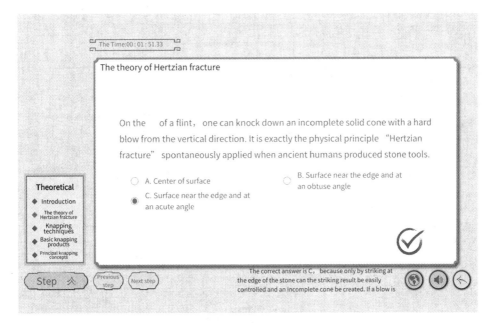

Figure 1-10    Choice Question About the Theory of Hertzian Fracture

## 1.2.3    Knapping Techniques

### ◎ Experimental Theory:

A technique refers to the practical manner of accomplishing a particular task. We define a "technique" as one of the procedures in manufacturing a craft (and sometimes an art), e.g. lithic artifacts of the prehistoric knapper. Examples of techniques include: direct percussion with a hammerstone, the *débitage* of a blade by pressure-flaking, and the fracture of a bladelet by means of the microburin blow (Inizan et al., 1999, pp. 156-157). Common techniques include freehand technique, anvil technique, bipolar-on-anvil technique, throwing technique, and pressure technique. Technique corresponds to the lower-most level of knowledge in the lithic technological system.

### ◎ Experimental Steps:

Click "Next step" to study the knapping techniques in turn: freehand knapping, anvil technique, bipolar-on-anvil technique, throwing technique and pressure technique. Students will complete the multiple-choice questions to consolidate what they have learnt earlier (Figure 1-11).

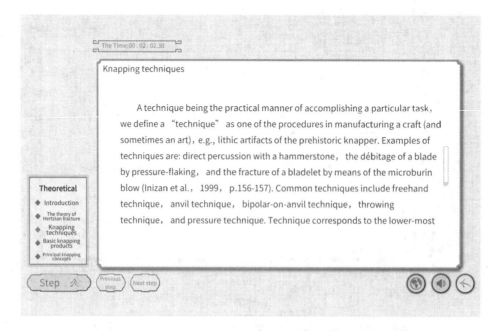

Figure 1-11    Explanations of the Knapping Techniques

(1) Freehand technique.

Freehand technique is the process of using a hammer and concentrating on a point on the surface of the stone near the edge to crack the stone with the help of the Hertzian cone principle. It can be used to process both flake blanks and tools. Depending on the presence or absence of an intermediary between the hammer and the raw material, this technique can be divided into: direct and indirect knapping (Figure 1-12).

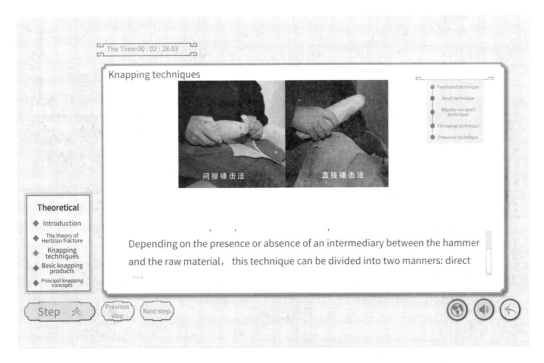

Figure 1-12    Schematic Representation and Interpretation of the Freehand Technique

(2) Anvil technique.

Anvil technique refers to the process of knapping a stone on another passive hammer, the anvil, in order to crack it (Figure 1-13).

(3) Bipolar-on-anvil technique.

Bipolar-on-anvil technique is the process of placing the stone on an anvil and using a hammer to fracture the stone at the right angle and with the right force (Figure 1-14).

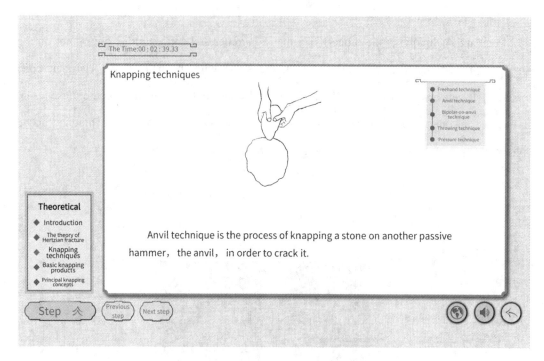

Figure 1-13    Schematic Representation and Interpretation of the Anvil Technique

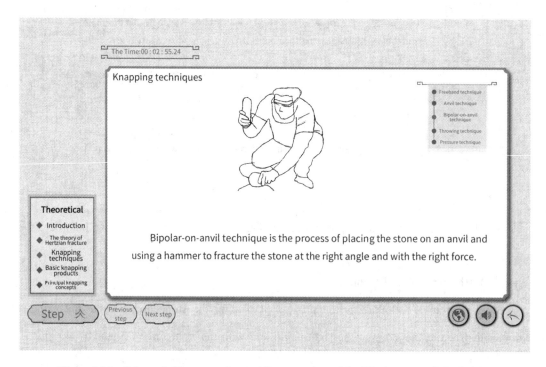

Figure 1-14    Schematic Representation and Interpretation of the Bipolar-on-anvil Technique

（4）Throwing technique.

Throwing technique is the process in which we fracture the stone by throwing it onto the anvil in a standing position (Figure 1-15).

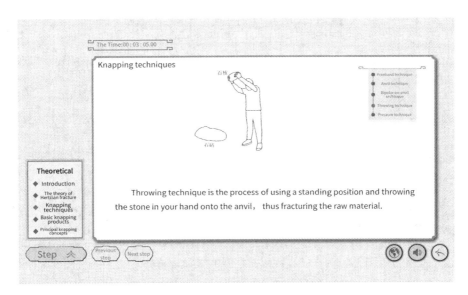

Figure 1-15　Schematic Representation and Interpretation of the Throwing Technique

（5）Pressure technique.

Unlike percussion, this technique of fracturing hard stone is carried out with a tool whose extremity applies pressure to detach a flake. Pressure can be used for *débitage* or retouching. (Figure 1-16).

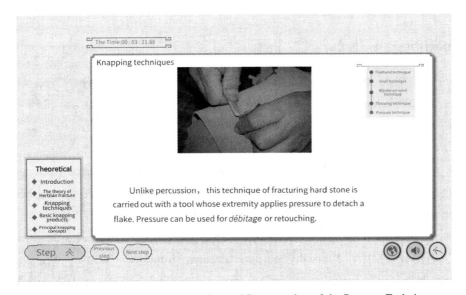

Figure 1-16　Schematic Representation and Interpretation of the Pressure Technique

Click "Next step" and answer the multiple choice question (Figure 1-17).

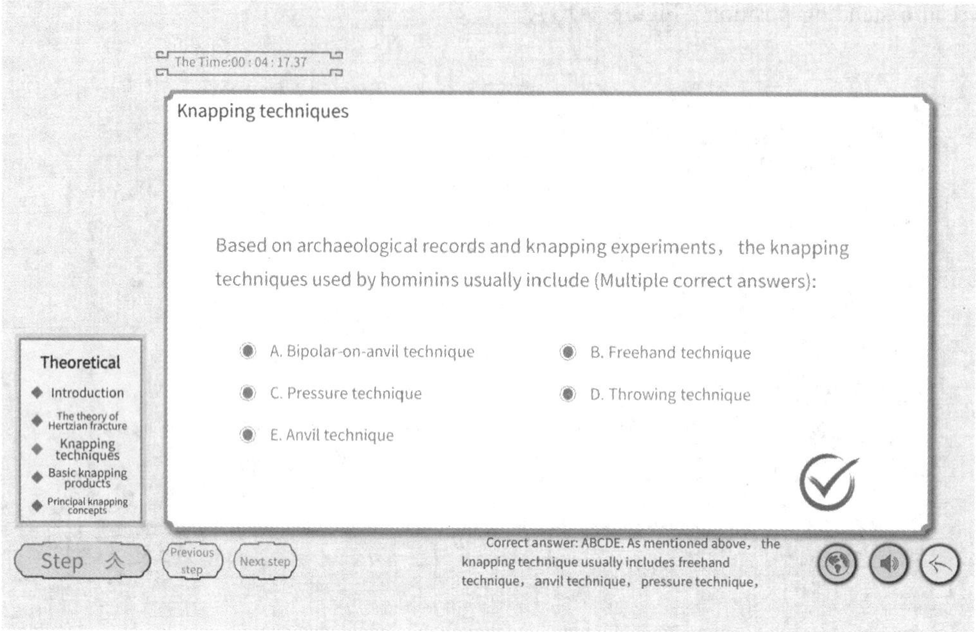

Figure 1-17    Multiple Choice Question About Knapping Techniques

## 1.2.4    Basic Knapping Products

### ▣ Raw Materials

### ◎ Experimental Steps:

Click on "Next step" to move on to the raw materials section, where you will learn about the three different types of raw materials with the help of pictures and 3D models of artifacts: cobble, limestone breccia, and vein nodules.

(1) Cobble.

The raw material selected by hominins for making stone tools was usually a natural rock with a smooth surface and no sharp edges, also known as river gravels. They are transported by water and more or less weathered after being deposited on the river bank; the surface roundness of these gravels varies from the distance and kinetic energy of water flow. The pebbles on river banks are usually transported away from their primary veins and are secondarily buried. Geologically, they are further classified as fine, coarse and massive gravels depending on their size. In Palaeolithic research, gravels are generally divided into small (pebble, <70 mm), large (cobble, ⩾70 mm) and giant (boulder, ⩾25 cm) (Figure 1-18).

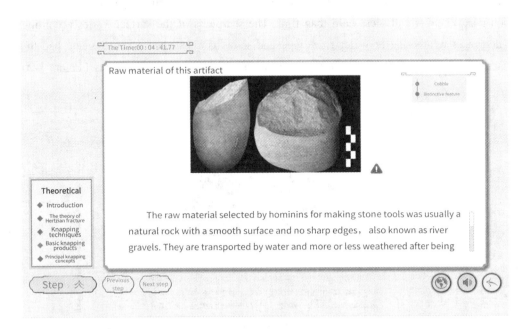

Figure 1-18　Photo and Interpretation of Cobble

Click Next step to learn about the distinctive feature of cobble (Figure 1-19).

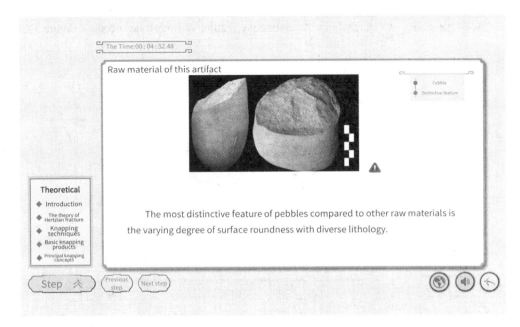

Figure 1-19　The Distinctive Feature of Cobble

（2）Limestone breccia.

Limestone caves or rock shelters often contain blocks that have been spalled down due to weathering and other causes. The main mineral compositions include carbonate and calcite, which make them slightly less hard than flint. The sharpness of the surface varies according to the degree of weathering or water rounding, and some have calcareous cements attached to the surface. Hominins used to select suitable limestone blocks for making stone tools (Figure 1-20).

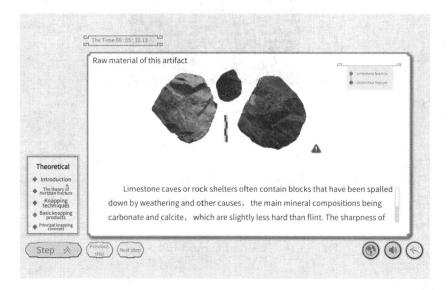

Figure 1-20    Explanation of Limestone Breccia

Click "Next step" to learn about the distinctive feature of limestone breccia (Figure 1-21).

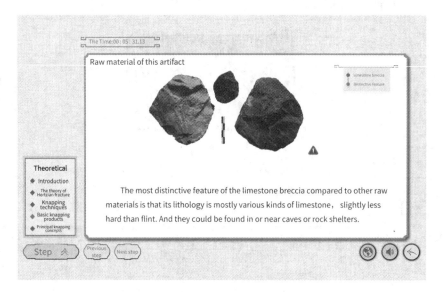

Figure 1-21    The Distinctive Feature of Limestone Breccia

（3）Vein nodules.

Vein nodules are raw materials exploited by hominins in mountainous rock-strip accumulations for use in the making of stone tools. Geologically, they are mineral aggregates that differ significantly from the surrounding rock in terms of composition, structure and colour and have a clear interface with the surrounding rock. They are often developed in the rock formations of mountain ranges. What was mined by the ancient humans were usually relatively homogeneous, isotropic clasts or nodules exposed and spalled from these mineral assemblages by weathering or other causes. They have not been transported by water or wind and were buried *in situ* (Figure 1-22).

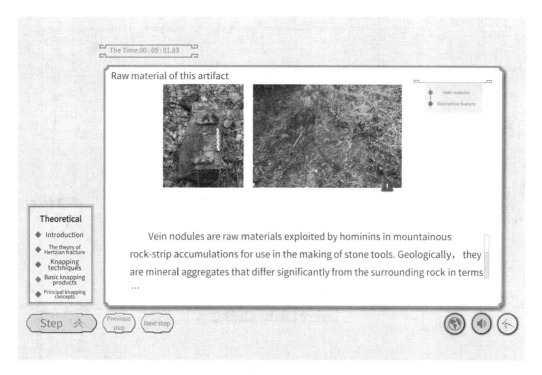

Figure 1-22    Definition of Vein Nodules

Click "Next step" to learn about the distinctive feature of vein nodules (Figure 1-23).

（4）Undetermined.

It is difficult to determine the initial form as the natural surface of the raw material has been removed (Figure 1-24).

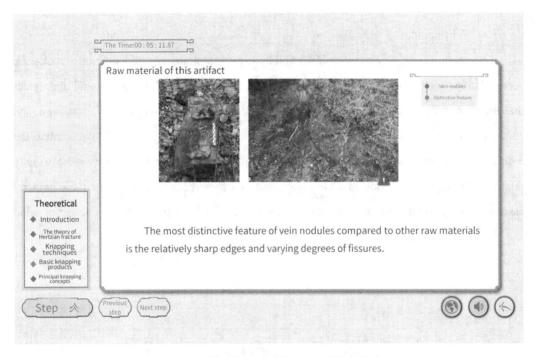

Figure 1-23   The Distinctive Feature of Vein Nodules

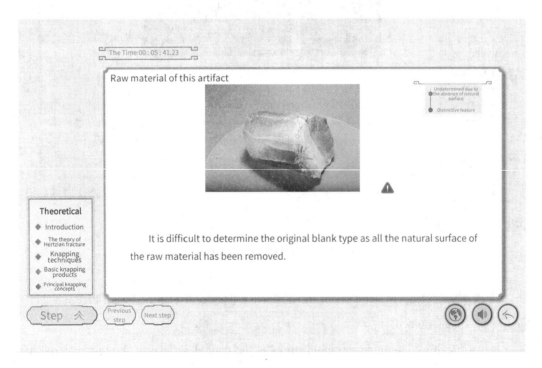

Figure 1-24   Undetermined Raw Material Type

Click "Next step" to learn about the distinctive feature of undetermined type (Figure 1-25).

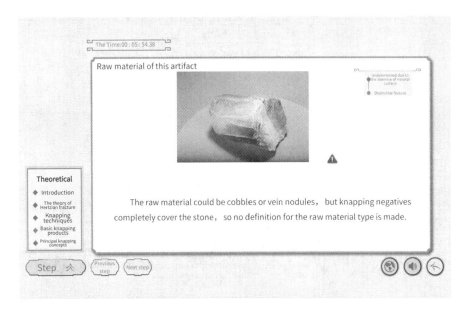

Figure 1-25    Example of the Undetermined Type

Click on "Next step" to proceed to the two multiple choice questions and read explanations (Figure 1-26—Figure 1-27).

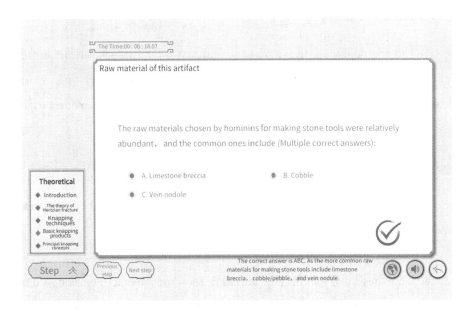

Figure 1-26    First Multiple Choice Question About Raw Material Type

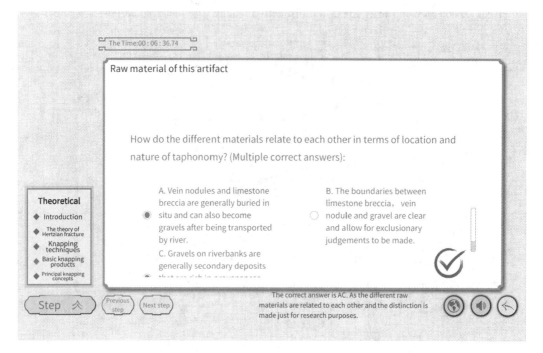

Figure 1-27　Second Multiple Choice Question About Raw Material Type

## The Surface Condition of the Stones

◎ **Experimental Theory:**

According to the degree of freshness and sharpness of the ridges on the surface, and taking into account the burial context of the lithic artifacts, researchers often classify the surface condition of the stones into three classes: no obvious abrasion, moderate abrasion, and heavy abrasion.

◎ **Experimental Steps:**

Click "Next step" to learn how to judge the degree of abrasion based on the surface state of the stones.

(1) No obvious abrasion.

The edges are fresh and sharp, and the scars show no obvious abrasion, collision or weathering, suggesting that the artifact was not subjected to significant geological actions after being discarded (Figure 1-28).

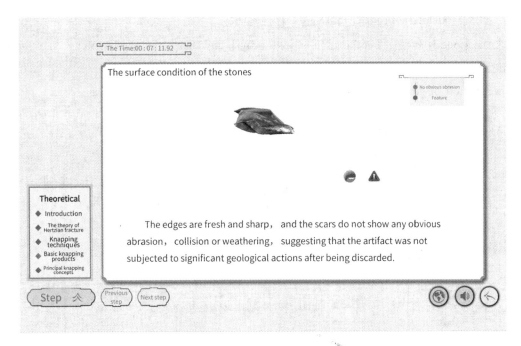

Figure 1-28　Definition of no Obvious Abrasion

Click "Next step" to learn more about its feature (Figure 1-29).

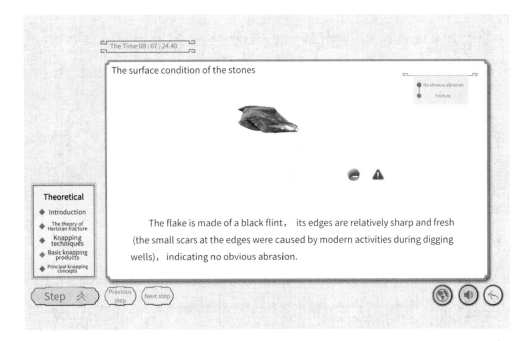

Figure 1-29　Feature of no Obvious Abrasion

（2）Moderate abrasion.

The stone is angular but the edge is not too fresh and sharp, and the knapping scars show some degree of abrasion, impact and weathering, suggesting that the artifact was subjected to a short period of geological action after being discarded (Figure 1-30).

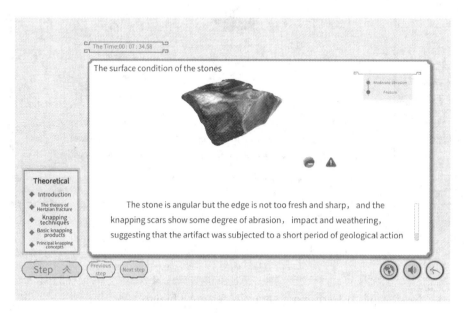

Figure 1-30   Definition of Moderate Abrasion

Click "Next step" to learn more about the feature of moderate abrasion (Figure 1-31).

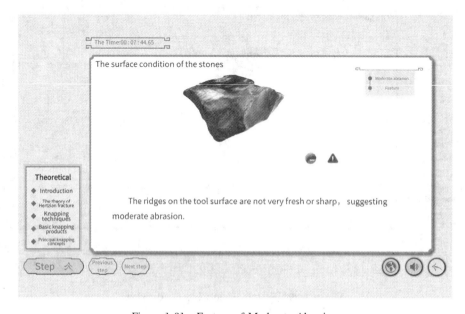

Figure 1-31   Feature of Moderate Abrasion

（3）Heavy abrasion.

The surface angles of the stone are no longer protruding and have become rounded, and the knapping scars have been significantly smoothed, suggesting that the artifact was subjected to a long period of geological action after being buried (Figure 1-32).

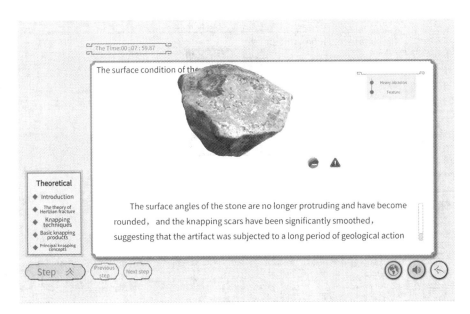

Figure 1-32   Definition of Heavy Abrasion

Click "Next step" to learn more about the feature of heavy abrasion (Figure 1-33).

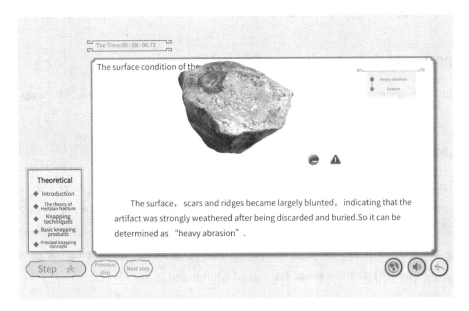

Figure 1-33   Feature of Heavy Abrasion

Click "Next step" and a choice question and related explanation will be displayed (Figure 1-34).

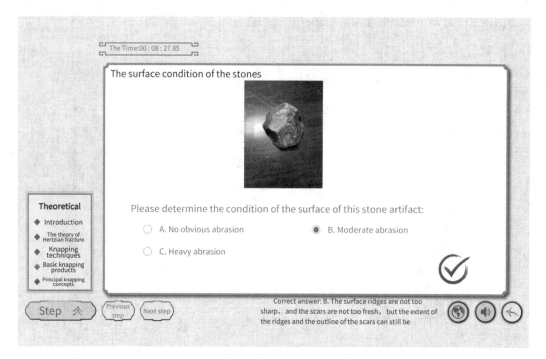

Figure 1-34　Choice Question About Surface Condition Determination

## Theoretical Study of Flakes

◎ **Experimental Principles:**

Learn the technical elements of flakes through textual explanations, pictures or 3D models.

◎ **Experimental Steps:**

After entering the interface of the theoretical study of flakes, click "Next step" to learn the definition of flakes, classification of flake butts, classification of flake dorsal face types, orientation and layout conventions of flakes, measurement of flakes, and judgement of knapping direction of flakes based on the photos and 3D models. After the section about basic concepts is completed, choice questions should be finished.

(1) Flake.

Flake is a general term for a fragment that is removed from a hard stone: either from a core or from a cobble or a tool, etc. Because of the Hertzian fracture, flakes have similar recognizable features, including butt/striking platform, point of impact, bulb, waves/ripples, dorsal face, ventral face, flaking angle, flaking direction, hackles (Figure 1-35 – Figure 1-44).

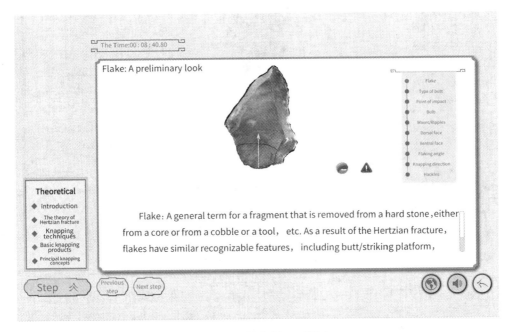

Figure 1-35　Definition of Flake

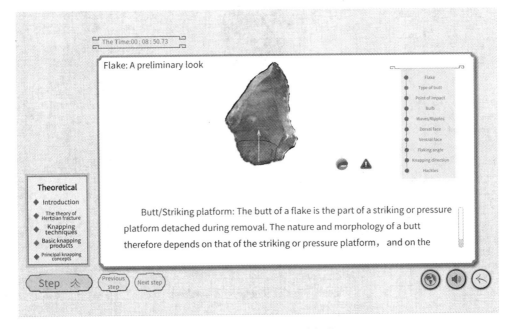

Figure 1-36　Definition of Flake Butt

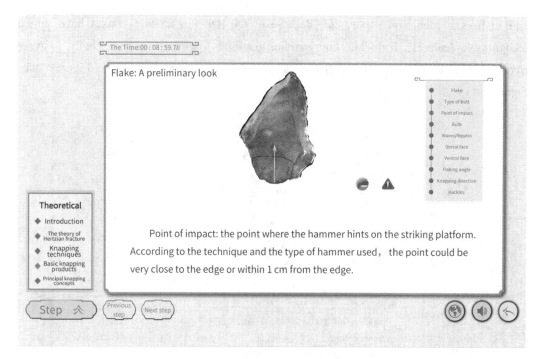

Figure 1-37    Definition of Impact Point

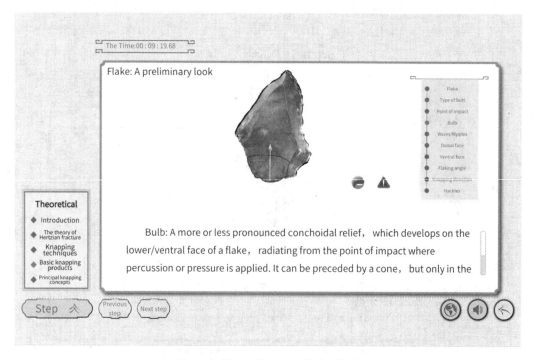

Figure 1-38    Definition of Flake Bulb

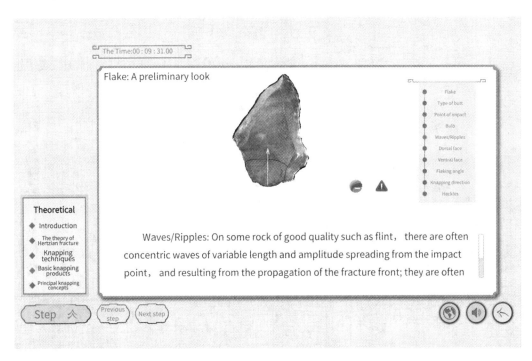

Figure 1-39 Definition of Ripples/Waves

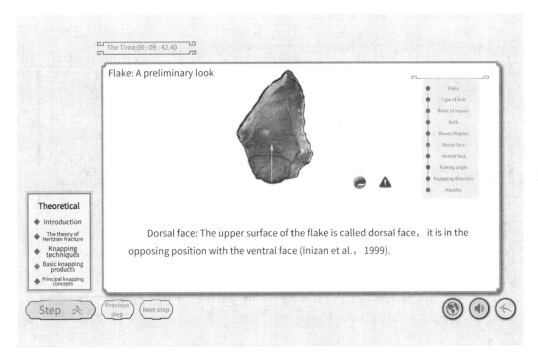

Figure 1-40 Definition of Dorsal Face

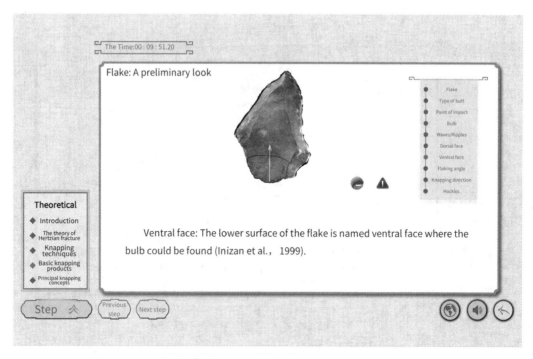

Figure 1-41　Definition of Ventral Face

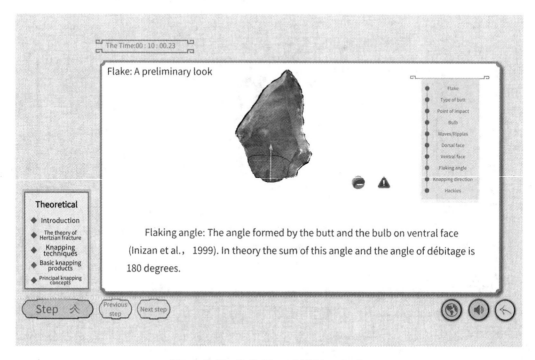

Figure 1-42　Definition of Flaking Angle

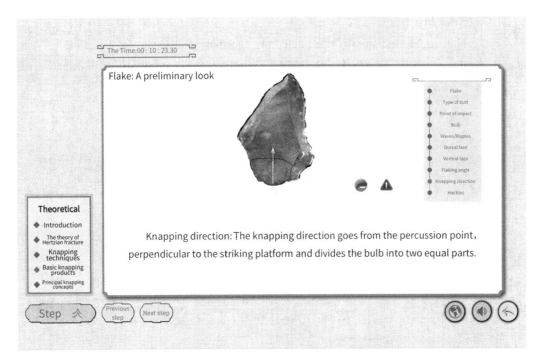

Figure 1-43   Definition of Knapping Direction

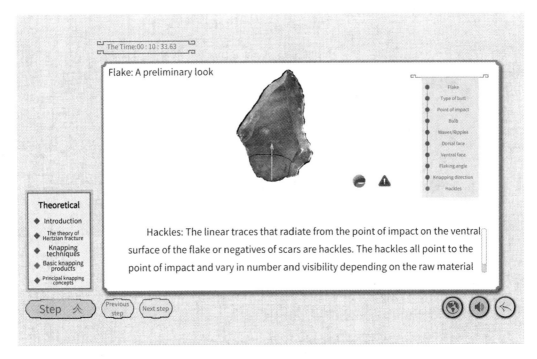

Figure 1-44   Definition of Hackles

（2）Flake butt types.

Flake butt could be natural, flat, dihedral, facetted, "chapeau de gendarme", spur-like, punctiform and linear. Click "Next step" in turn to learn more about these butt types (Figure 1-45－Figure 1-52).

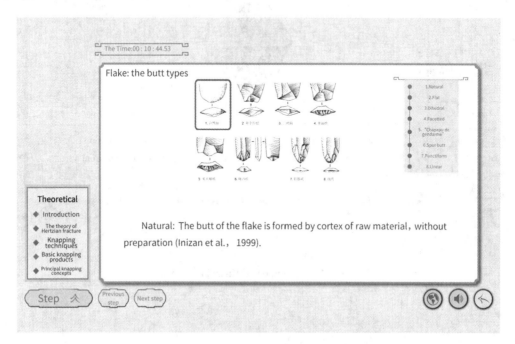

Figure 1-45   Natural Butt

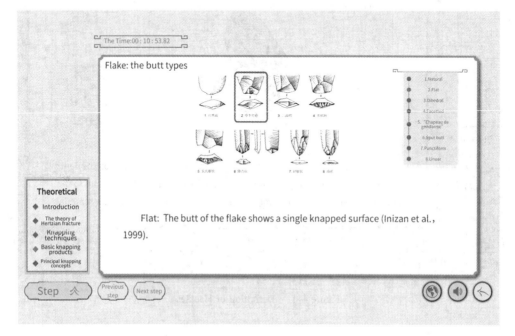

Figure 1-46   Flat Butt

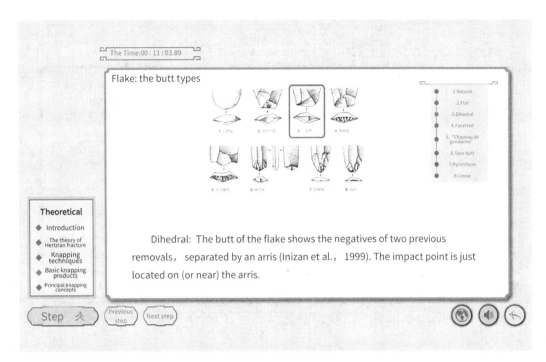

Figure 1-47 Dihedral Butt

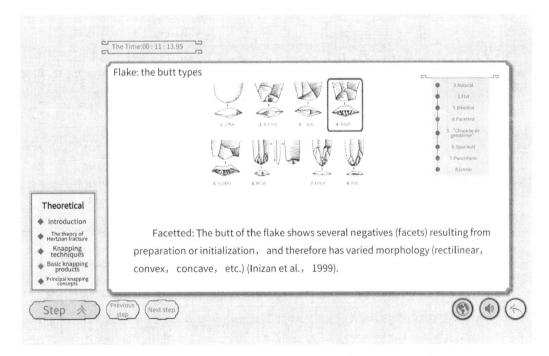

Figure 1-48 Facetted Butt

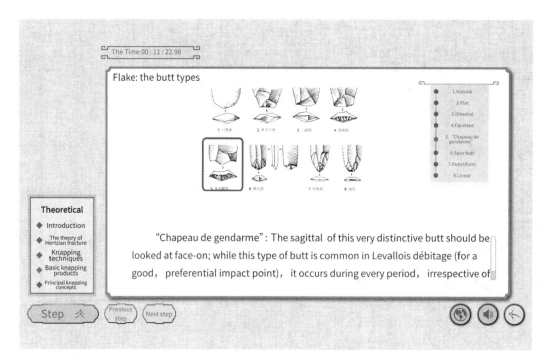

Figure 1-49 "Chapeau de Gendarme" Butt

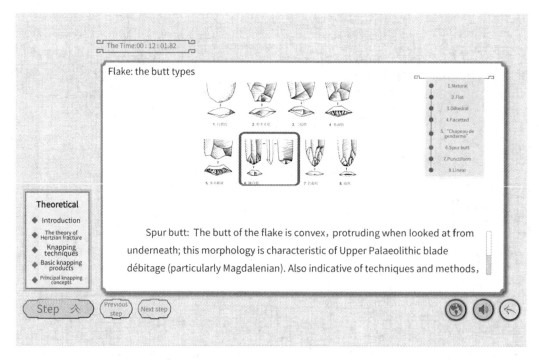

Figure 1-50 Spur Butt

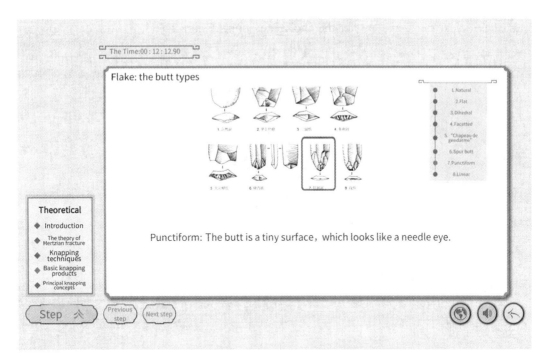

Figure 1-51　Punctiform Butt

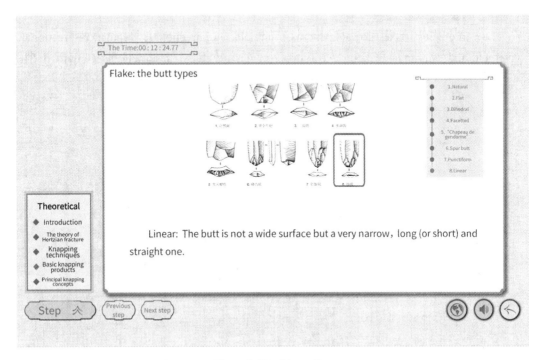

Figure 1-52　Linear Butt

Click "Next step" and answer the choice question (Figure 1-53).

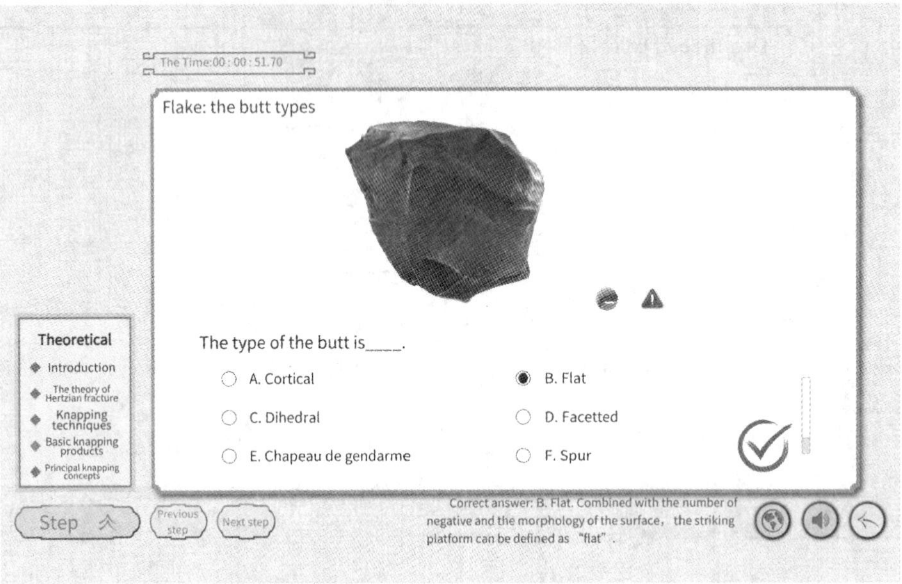

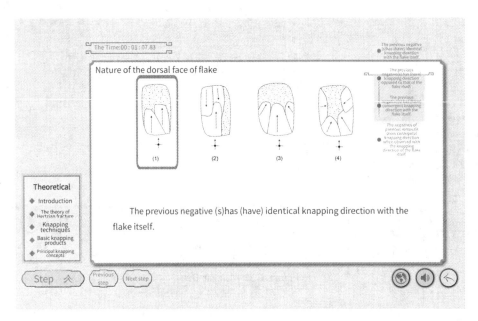

Figure 1-53  Determination of the Flake Butt Type

(3) Flake dorsal patterns.

There are four flake dorsal patterns: unipolar/unidirectional, bipolar/bidirectional, convergent and centripetal. Click "Next step" in turn to study these patterns (Figure 1-54 – Figure 1-57).

Figure 1-54  Unipolar or Unidirectional Dorsal Pattern

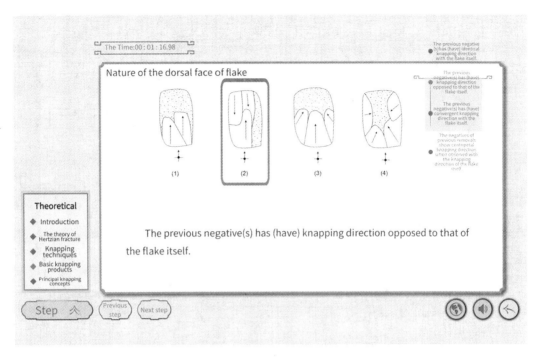

Figure 1-55 Bipolar or Bidirectional Dorsal Pattern

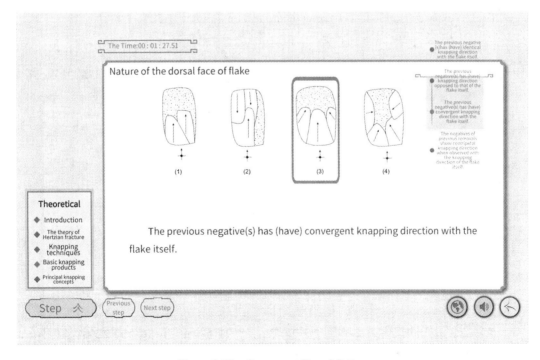

Figure 1-56 Convergent Dorsal Pattern

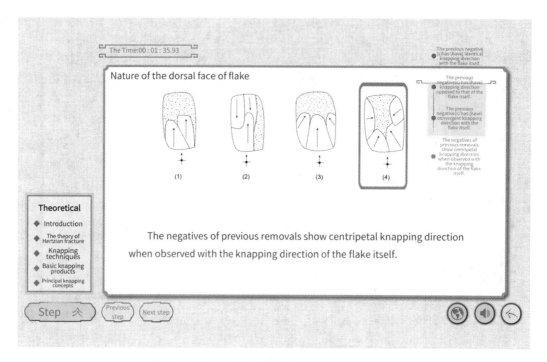

Figure 1-57   Centripetal Dorsal Pattern

Click "Next step" and answer the choice question (Figure 1-58).

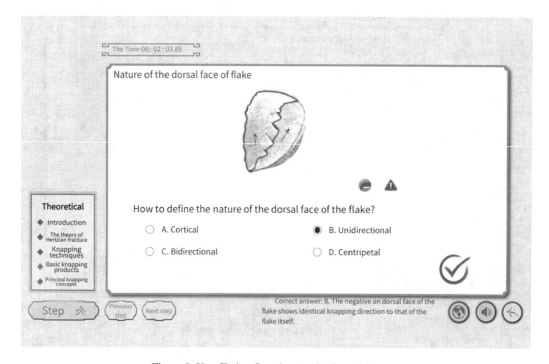

Figure 1-58   Choice Question on the Dorsal Pattern

（4）Orientation and layout conventions for flakes.

Based on what you have learnt earlier, please complete its right positioning of the flake by pressing the right mouse button, grabbing and rotating the 3D model of the artifact (Figure 1-59).

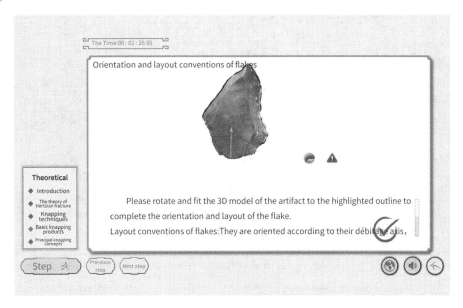

Figure 1-59　Orientation and Layout Conventions for Flakes

Click "Next step" and complete its right positioning of the flake by pressing the right mouse button, grabbing and rotating the 3D model of the artifact (Figure 1-60).

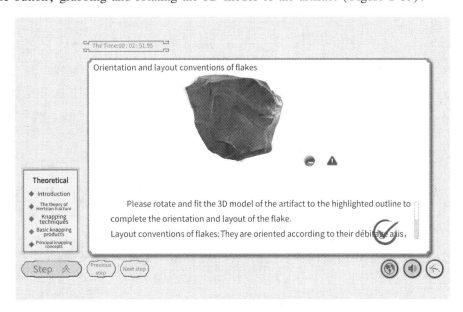

Figure 1-60　Practicing Orientation and Layout Conventions for Flakes

（5）Measurement of flakes or scars.

Use the vernier calipers in the toolbar on the right side of the page, and zoom in or zoom out the buttons to measure the length and width of the specimen, which are then filled in the dialogue box that pops up. Also learn the meaning of descriptive terms such as proximal part, distal part, middle part, left part, and right part of a flake (Figure 1-61−Figure 1-67).

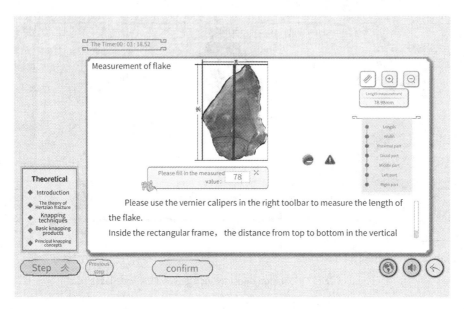

Figure 1-61   Measuring the Length of a Flake

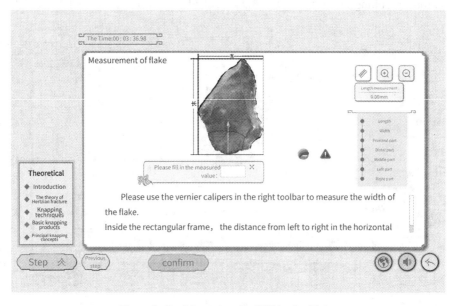

Figure 1-62   Measuring the Width of a Flake

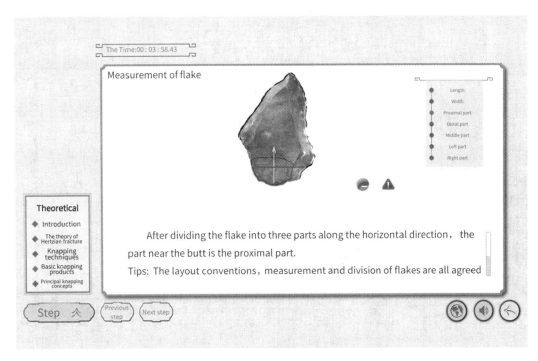

Figure 1-63　The Proximal Part of a Flake

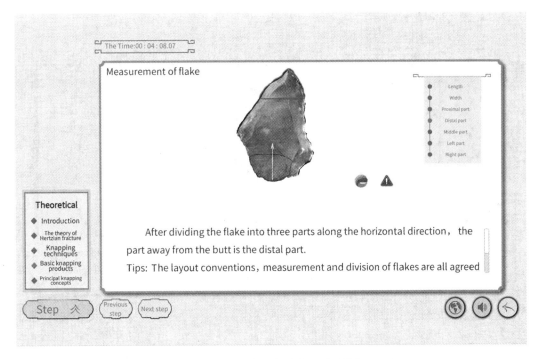

Figure 1-64　The Distal Part of a Flake

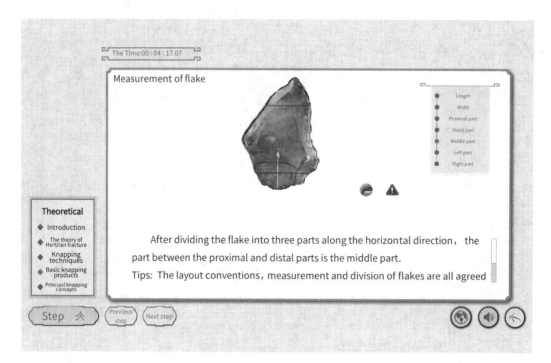

Figure 1-65　The Mesial Part of a Flake

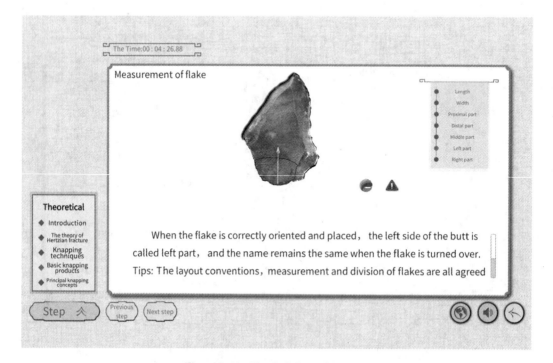

Figure 1-66　The Left Part of a Flake

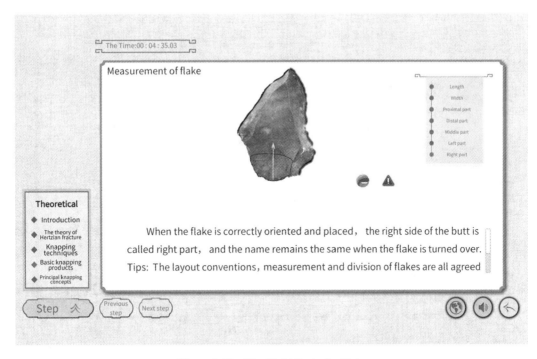

Figure 1-67　The Right Part of a Flake

Click "Next step" and answer the choice question (Figure 1-68–Figure 1-69).

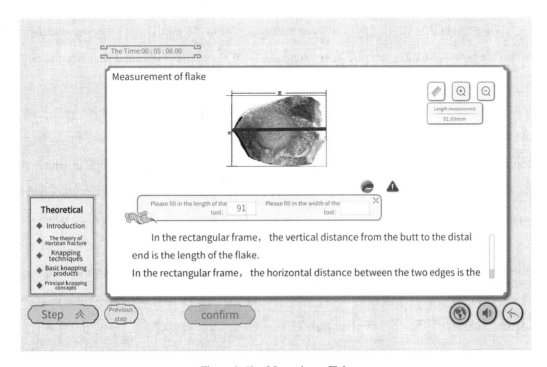

Figure 1-68　Measuring a Flake

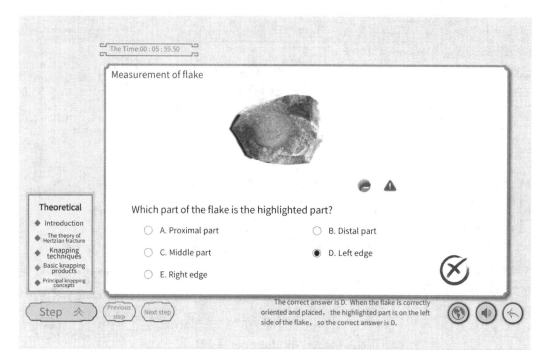

Figure 1-69   Choice Question About the Different Parts of a Flake

(6) Identifying the knapping direction of the flake and negatives.

When the butt is visible, the direction perpendicular to the butt is the knapping direction. When the bulb is visible, the direction extending from the impact point and dividing the bulb in half, is the knapping direction of the flake. When waves/ripples are visible, the intersection of the mid-pipeline of the chords of two concentric waves is the impact point, and the direction originating from the impact point is the knapping direction under the condition of considering the overall shape of the flake. When the hackles are visible, the point at which all the hackles point is the impact point, and the direction originating from the impact point is the knapping direction under the condition of considering the overall shape of the flake. When the counter-bulb is visible, the proximal part of the counter-bulb is the impact point, and the direction extending from the impact point and dividing the bulb in half, is the knapping direction of the negative. Click "Next step" to understand the indicative meaning of each technical element (Figure 1-70−Figure 1-74).

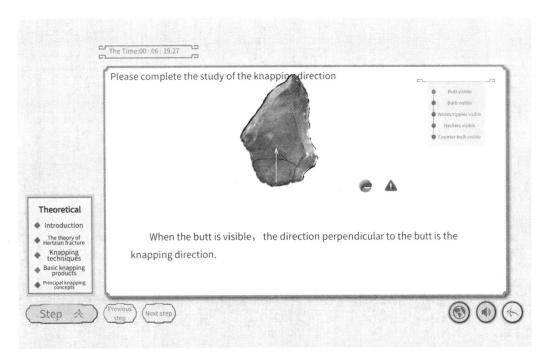

Figure 1-70   When the Butt is Visible

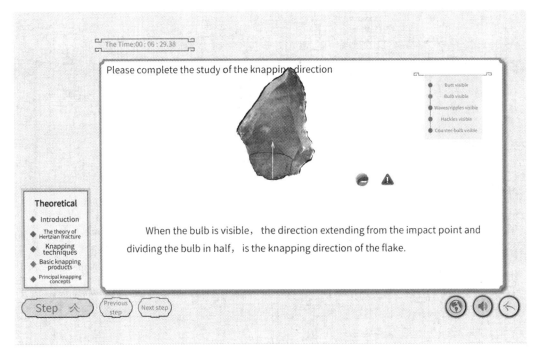

Figure 1-71   When the Bulb is Visible

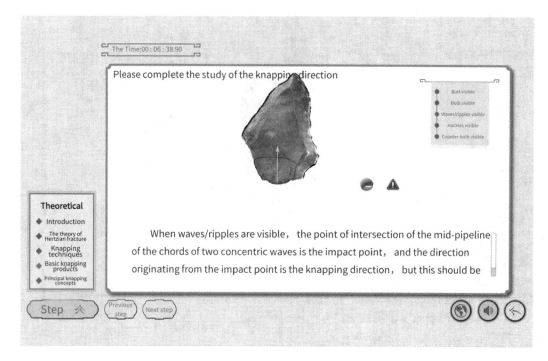

Figure 1-72    When the Waves/Ripples are Visible

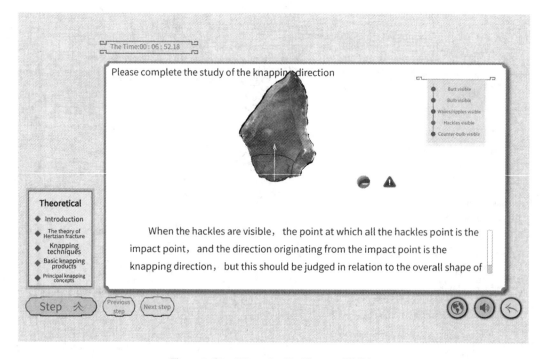

Figure 1-73    When the Hackles are Visible

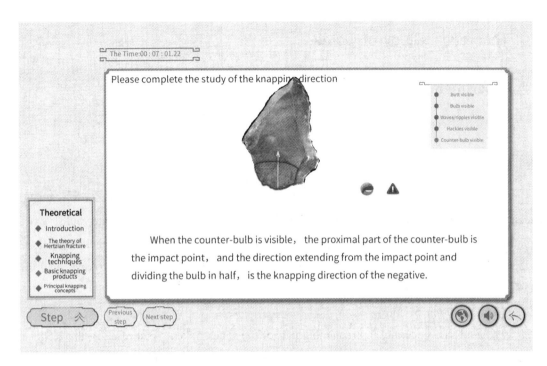

Figure 1-74　When the Counter-bulb is Visible

Click "Next" to complete the exercise (Figure 1-75).

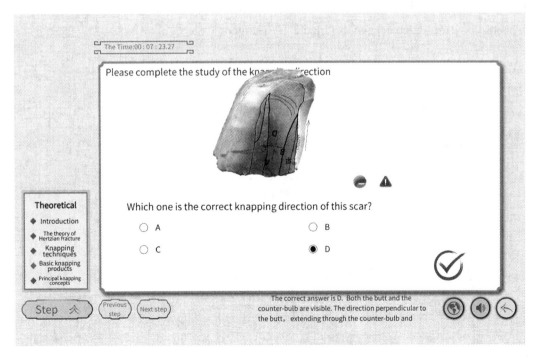

Figure 1-75　Choice Question About the Knapping Direction

## 🗒 Theoretical Study of Cores

### ◎ Experimental Principles:

Learn the technical elements of cores by photos and 3D models of artifacts.

### ◎ Experimental Steps:

Enter the interface of cores: A preliminary look. Click "Next step" in order to learn the technical elements of cores including striking platform, point of impact, counter-bulb, arris, platform angle (or exterior angle), surface of *débitage*, knapping direction, hackles, waves/ripples, etc. At the same time, learn the layout conventions of cores, striking platform determination and measurement of scars.

(1) Definition of cores.

The cores are generally the remaining part of the sones flaked. As a result of the Hertzian fracture principle, the surface of the core produces a number of recognizable features, including striking platform, impact point, counter-bulb, arrises, platform angle, surface of *débitage*, knapping direction, hackles, waves/ripples, etc. Theoretically the core and the flake are originated from one volume. The difference between the two is that the flake generally has a prominent bulb below the butt, while the corresponding location on the core is a depression, i.e., a counter-bulb (Figure 1-76−Figure 1-85).

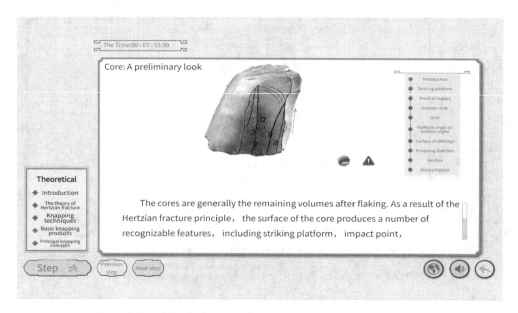

Figure 1-76    A Preliminary Look at the Technical Elements of Cores

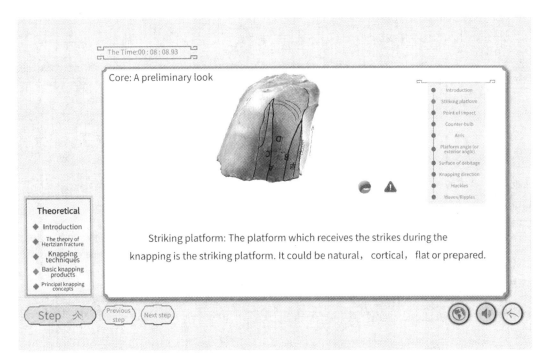

Figure 1-77　Definition of the Striking Platform

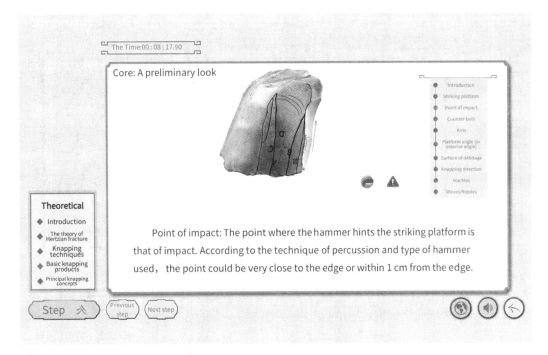

Figure 1-78　Definition of the Impact Point

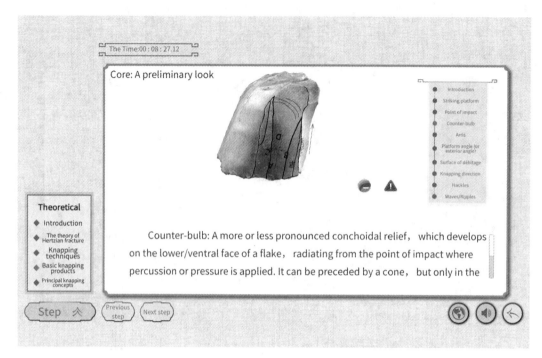

Figure 1-79    Definition of the Counter-bulb

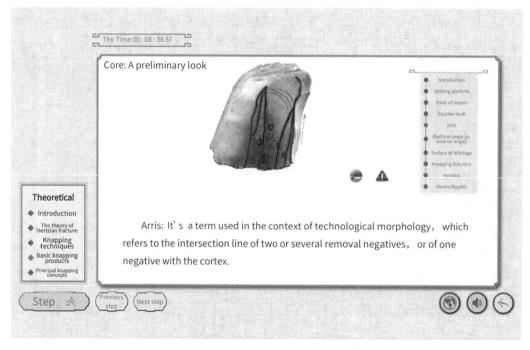

Figure 1-80    Definition of Arris

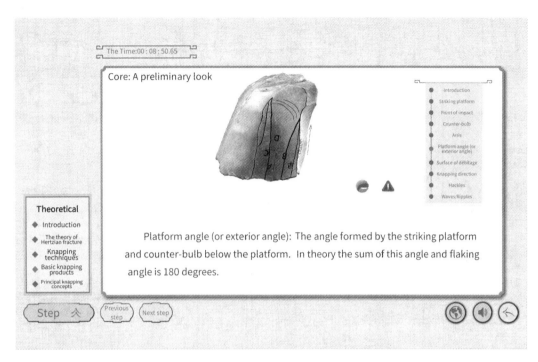

Figure 1-81 Definition of Platform Angle

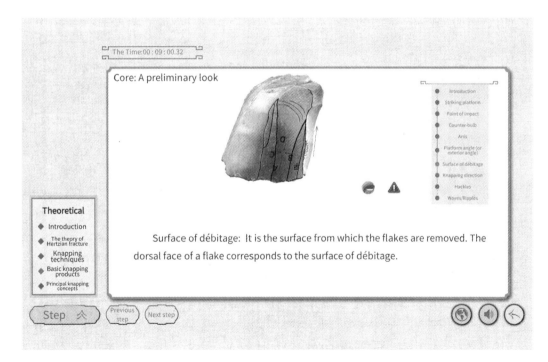

Figure 1-82 Definition of Surface of *Débitage*

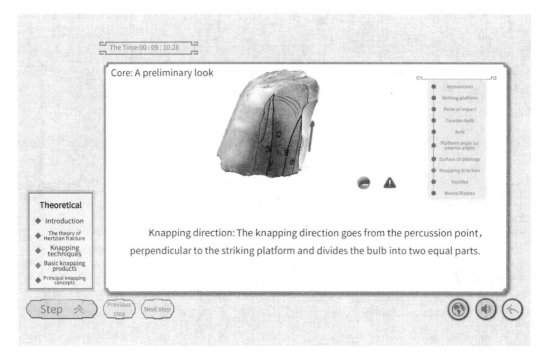

Figure 1-83   Definition of Knapping Direction

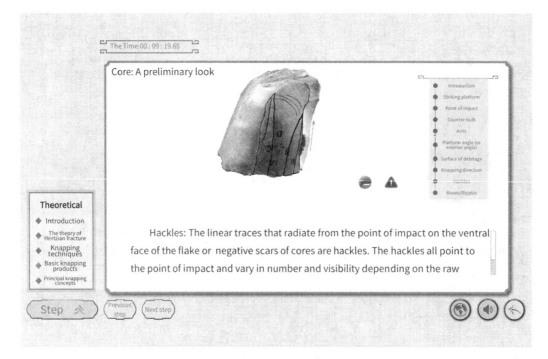

Figure 1-84   Definition of Hackles

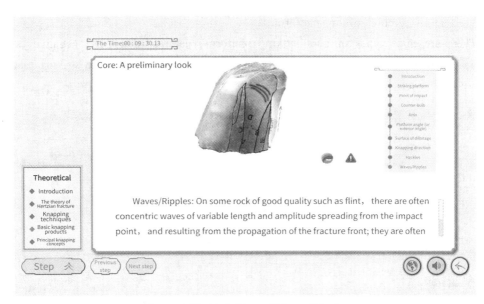

Figure 1-85  Definition of Waves/Ripples

（2）Layout conventions for cores.

There are no specific rules for the layout of cores. It depends on the result of technological analysis. If the striking platform of the last removal can be identified, the core can be oriented according to the *débitage* axis of the last removal, with the platform upward or downward. If the striking platform of the last removal cannot be identified, the core is oriented according to its morphology.

Please complete the test about the layout conventions for cores (Figure 1-86).

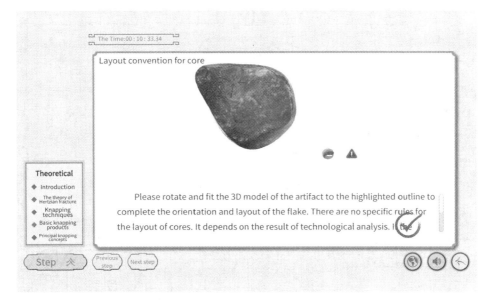

Figure 1-86  Test About the Layout Conventions for Cores

（3）Types of core striking platform.

There are three types of core striking platform: natural, diaclases, negative（s）of previous removal（s）. Please click "Next step" to study the types of the striking platform （Figure 1-87－Figure 1-90）.

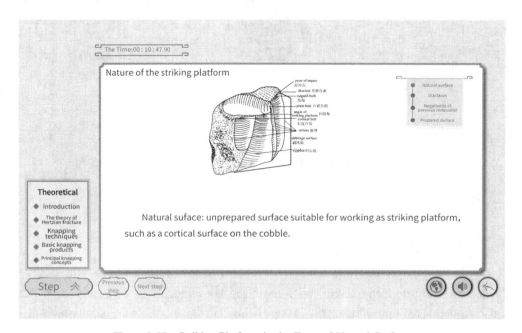

Figure 1-87    Striking Platform in the Form of Natural Surface

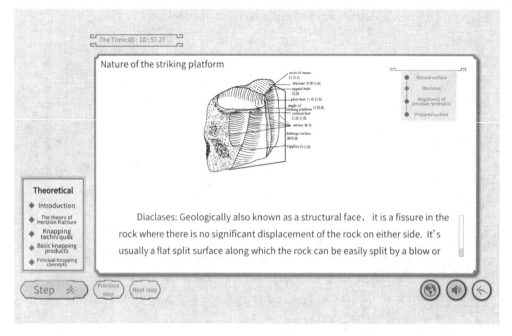

Figure 1-88    Striking Platform in the Form of Diaclases

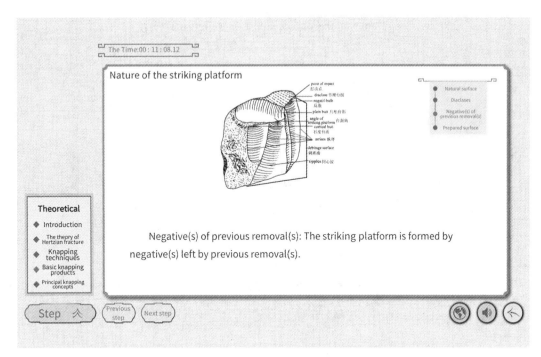

Figure 1-89　Striking Platform in the Form of Negative(s) of Previous Removal(s)

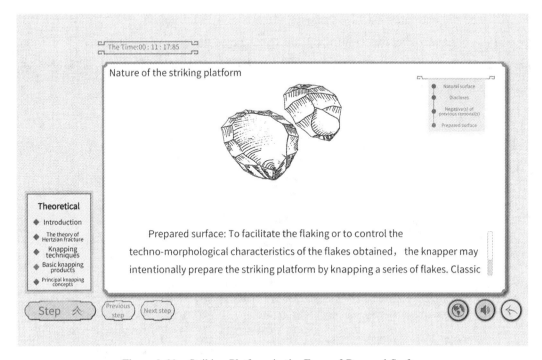

Figure 1-90　Striking Platform in the Form of Prepared Surface

Click "Next step" and answer the choice question (Figure 1-91).

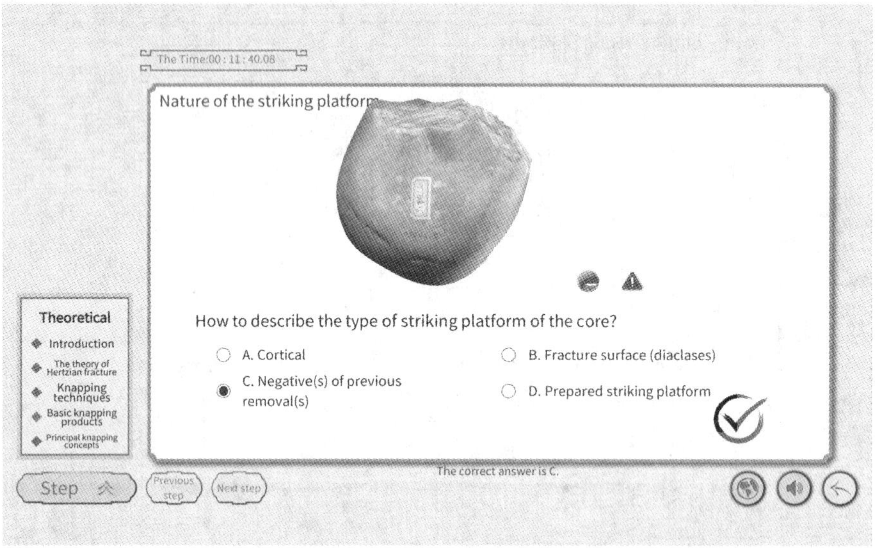

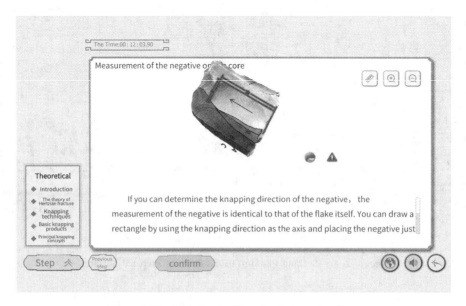

Figure 1-91    Choice Question About the Nature of Striking Platform

(4) Measurement of the negative scar on the core.

Change the placement of the 3D model of the core by adjusting the pre-labelled rectangle to face the observer; the area framed by the rectangle is the area of the negative scar to be measured. Follow the prompts to measure the length and width of the scar and fill in the data according to the system prompts (Figure 1-92).

Figure 1-92    Measure the Negative Scar on the Core

Click "Next step" to complete the choice question about the knapping direction of scars on cores (Figure 1-93).

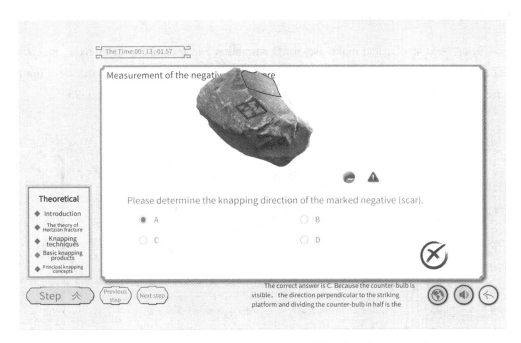

Figure 1-93　Choice Question on the Knapping Direction of a Certain Scar

Click "Next step" and complete the question (Figure 1-94).

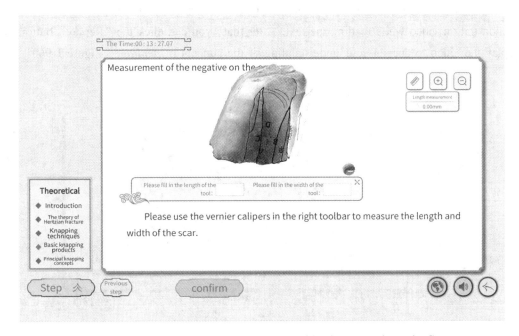

Figure 1-94　Measure the Negative Scar Framed by the Rectangle on the Core

## 1.2.5    Basic Productional Concepts

### ◎ Experimental Steps:

Click "Next step", and make use of 3D animation and textual explanations to understand what the concept of production is and the two concepts of production in the development course of the world's Palaeolithic technology: *débitage* and shaping (Figure 1-95).

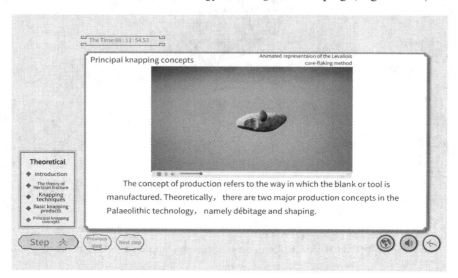

Figure 1-95    Basic Productional Concepts

(1) To learn the concept of *débitage*, click "Next step" and watch the 3D animated demonstration video while reading the text. After that, you can click the "Replay" button to replay the video to deepen your understanding of the concept of *débitage* (Figure 1-96).

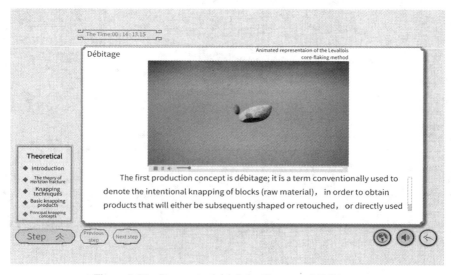

Figure 1-96    Demonstration of the Concept of *Débitage*

(2) To learn about the concept of shaping, click on "Next" and watch the 3D animated demonstration video while reading the text. After that, you can click the "Replay" button to replay the video to deepen your understanding of the concept of shaping (Figure 1-97).

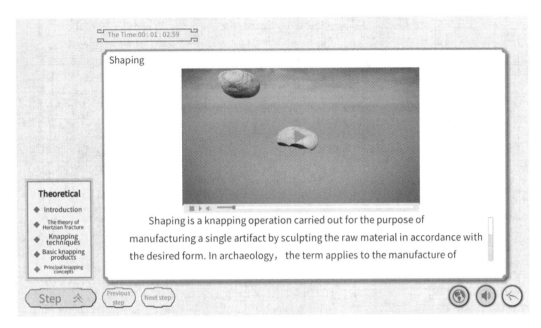

Figure 1-97   Demonstration of the Concept of Shaping

## 1.3   Refitting Experiments of Lithic Artifacts

Exit the "Theoretical study of lithic artifacts" module, select the "Refitting experiments of lithic artifacts" module, and go to the introduction to study the basic concepts of refitting analysis.

### 1.3.1   Introduction

Refitting (Conjoining): It involves reassembling the pieces or fragments into a coherent whole after their positive and negative knapping surfaces (débitage, retouch) or their fracture surfaces are identified, and then verifying that they are in fact complementary. It helps not only to reconstruct the knapping process and sequences and the site structure and taphonomic process, but also to understand spacial organization of hominins (Figure 1-98).

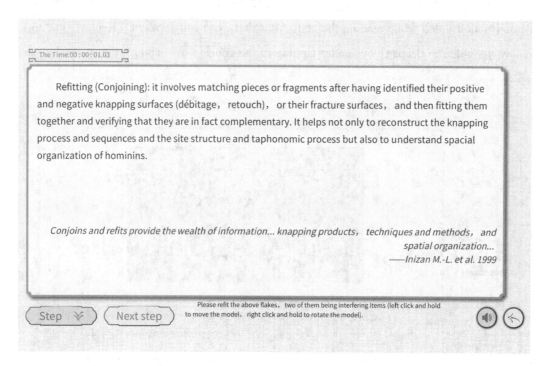

Figure 1-98   Definition of Refitting Analysis

## 1.3.2   Simple Refitting Experiments

### ◎ Experimental Steps:

Click "Next step" to enter the section of refitting; select 7 pieces from 10 artifacts according to their similarity in colour and texture, and compare the scar and the shape on the pieces to complete the refitting.

(1) Click the magnifying glass to observe all the stone artifacts; observationally select 7 stone artifacts of similar colour and texture from 10 artifacts (Figure 1-99).

(2) According to the observation, one core should be found out from the seven artifacts (Figure 1-100).

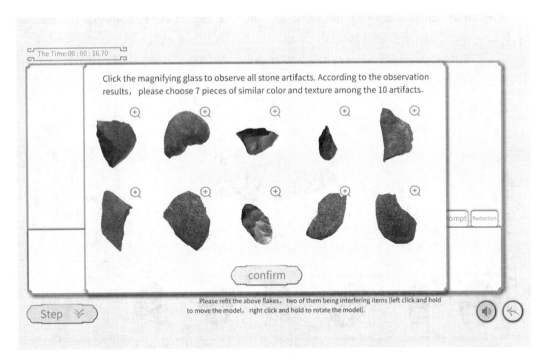

Figure 1-99 Refitting Stone Artifacts (Select Products)

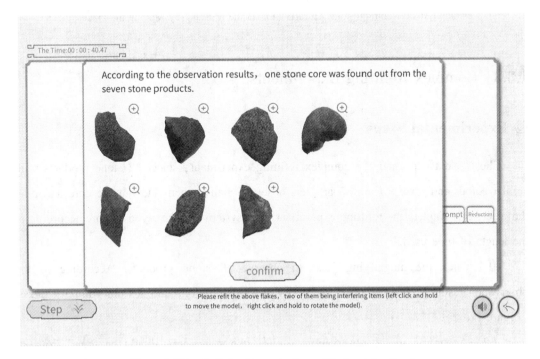

Figure 1-100 Refitting Stone Artifacts (Find out the Core)

(3) Grab, move and rotate the stone artifacts with the mouse to complete the refitting (Figure 1-101).

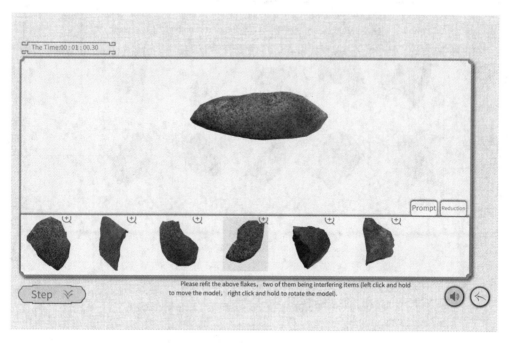

Figure 1-101  Refitting Stone Artifacts (Finish the Refitting by Moving the Flakes)

## 1.3.3  Complex Refitting Experiments

◎ **Experimental Steps:**

Click "Next" to enter the complex refitting experiment; select 32 stone products with similar colour and texture from 35 artifacts observationally, then find out the core and drag the pieces to complete the refitting experiment. The system will give you a score according to the length of time used.

(1) Click the magnifying glass to observe all stone products. According to the observation results, please choose 32 pieces of similar colour and texture from 35 pieces (Figure 1-102).

(2) According to the observation results, one stone core should be found from 32 artifacts (Figure 1-103).

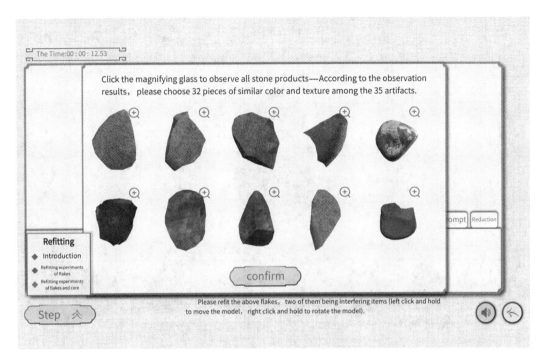

Figure 1-102　Complex Refitting（Select Artifacts）

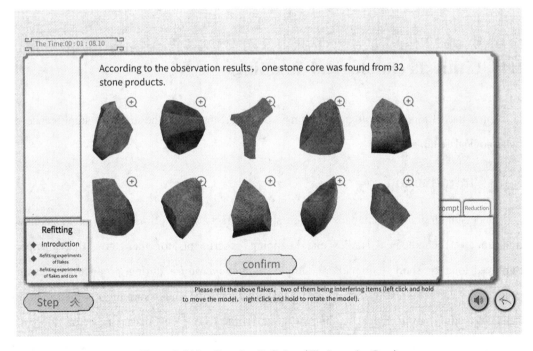

Figure 1-103　Complex Refitting（Find out the Core）

（3）Drag the flakes in order onto the core to finish the refitting（Figure 1-104）.

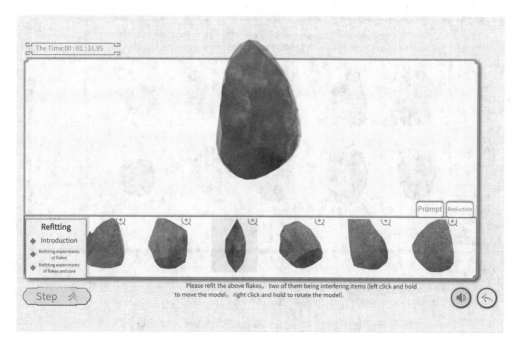

Figure 1-104　Complex Refitting（Finish the Refitting）

## 1.4　Lithic Technological Reading

Enter the "Lithic technological reading" module, and study the aim and significance of technological reading.

### 1.4.1　Introduction

Understanding ancient humans through stone artifacts is the primary goal of Palaeolithic archaeology. Technological studies and knapping experiments together show that knappers employed long or short, complex or simple *chaîne opératoire* during production of stone tools, and were governed by certain ideas and intentions, the understanding of which requires technical reading. By technical reading of stone artifacts, one can master a set of rules that allow systematic and scientific observation, deconstruction and perception of ancient human behaviors and cognitive modes（Figure 1-105）.

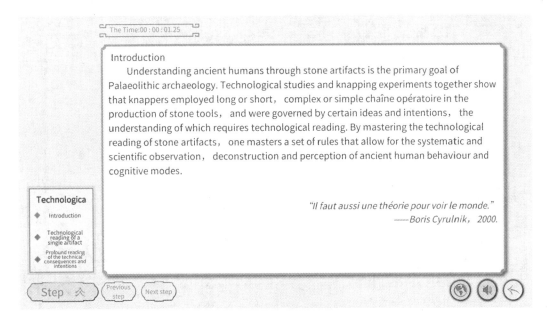

Figure 1-105　Introduction to Technological Reading

## 1.4.2　Technological Reading of a Single Artifact

◎ **Experimental Steps:**

Click "Next step" or the title in the sidebar in order to go to the technical reading of the artifact.

(1) Raw material.

Based on what you have learnt before, rotate and zoom the 3D model of the artifact to determine the type of raw material. The system will determine if the answer is correct or incorrect and give an explanation (Figure 1-106).

(2) Surface condition of the stone artifact.

Based on what have learnt before, rotate and zoom the 3D model to determine the surface condition of the artifact. The system will determine if the answer is correct or incorrect and give an explanation (Figure 1-107).

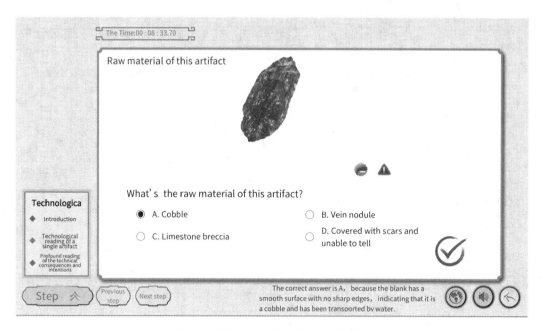

Figure 1-106　Raw Material Identification

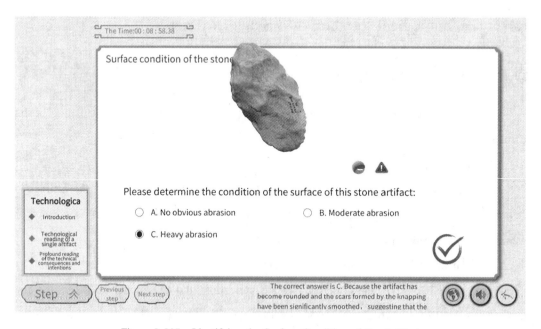

Figure 1-107　Identifying the Surface Condition of the Artifact

(3) Identification of the knapping direction.

Based on what you have learnt before, rotate and zoom the 3D model to determine the knapping direction of the marked scar on the artifact. The system will determine if the answer is correct or incorrect and give an explanation (Figure 1-108).

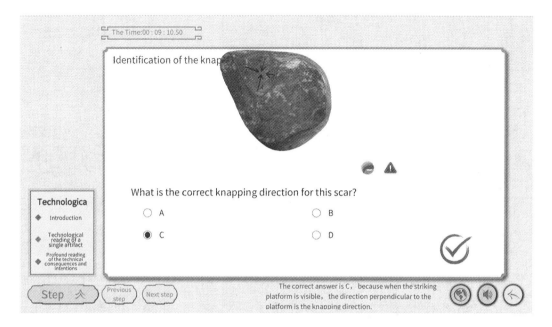

Figure 1-108   Identifying the Knapping Direction of the Marked Scar

(4) Identification of the knapping order.

Click "Next step" and learn the technical characteristics indicating the knapping order of scars: 1) the degree of weathering and abrasion of the scars; 2) the completeness of intersecting scars; 3) the degree of prickliness of the intersecting ridge; 4) the principle of irreversible chronological order; 5) difference in depth of unidirectional scars; 6) visibility of the counter-bulbs of intersecting scars; 7) visibility of the hackles, etc. (Figure 1-109−Figure 1-114).

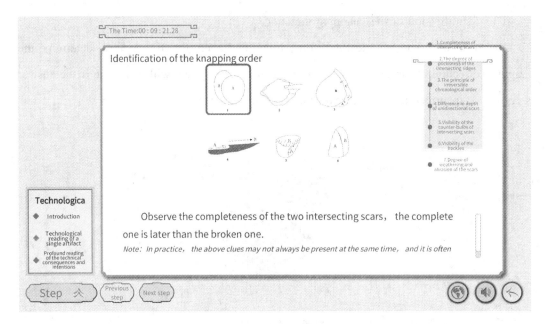

Figure 1-109   Completeness of Two Intersecting Scars Indicating Knapping Order

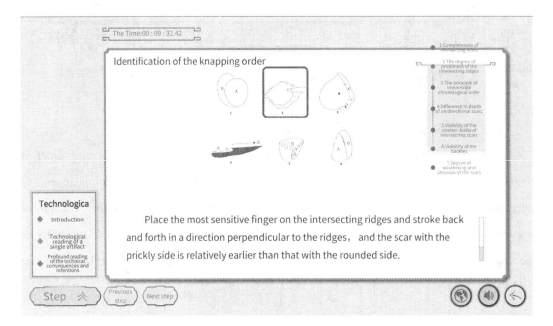

Figure 1-110   The Degree of Prickliness of the Intersecting Ridge Indicating the Knapping Order

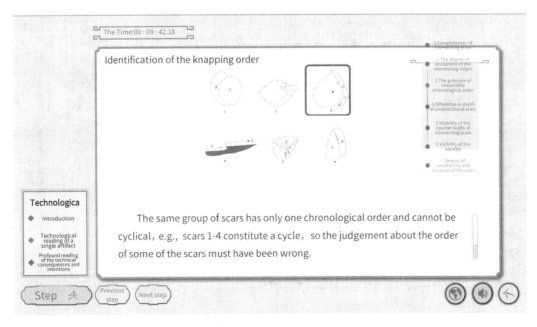

Figure 1-111   Schematic Illustration of the Principle of Irreversible Chronological Order

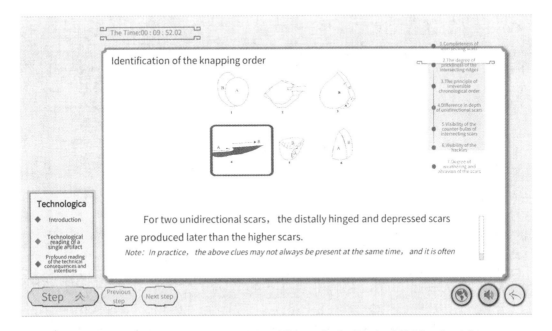

Figure 1-112   Schematic Illustration of the Difference in the Depth of Unidirectional Scars

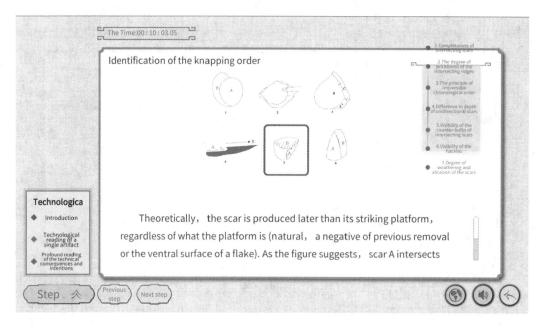

Figure 1-113    Schematic Illustration of the Visibility of the Counter-Bulbs of Intersecting Scars Indicating

Their Chronological Order

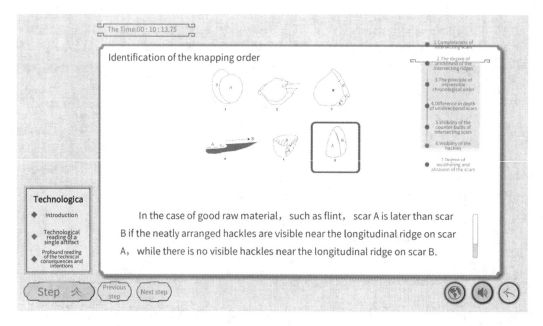

Figure 1-114    Schematic Illustration of the Visibility of the Hackles Indicating Their Chronological Order

Click "Next step" and answer the choice question (Figure 1-115).

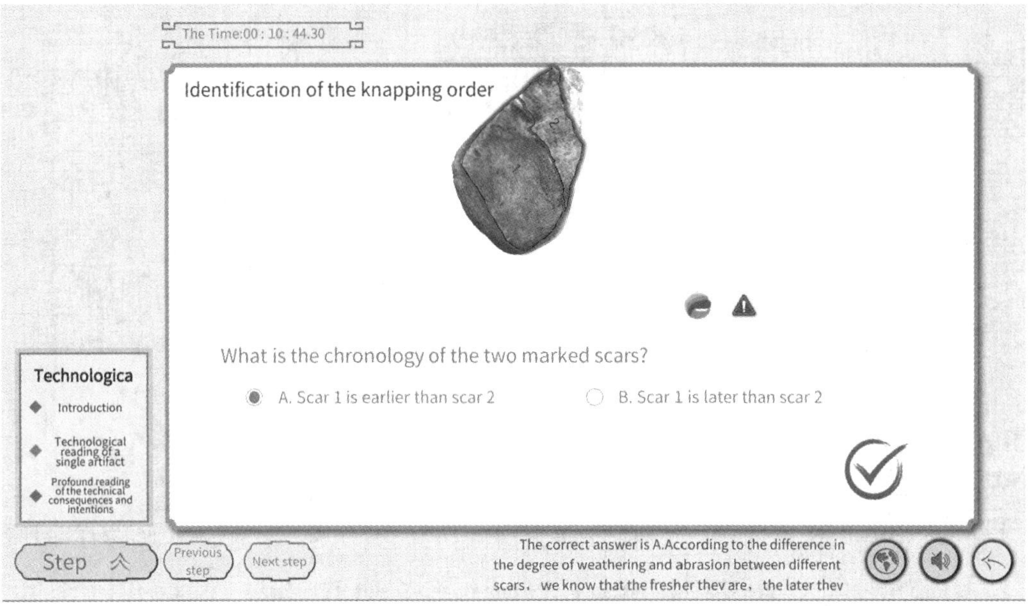

Figure 1-115   Choice Question About the Determination of Knapping Order

## 1.4.3   Further Reading of the Technical Consequences and Intentions

◎ **Experimental Steps:**

(1) Identification of the *débitage* system.

Click "Next step" and enter the "Further reading of the technical consequences and intentions" section. First, complete the task of identifying the core flaking system by rotating and zooming the 3D model of the artifact. Analyze the striking platform, lateral convexities, and distal convexity, and then get a conclusion about the flaking system. Four choice questions need to be answered. Students will learn about the flaking system during these observations. This section provides three core flaking systems, i.e., simple core flaking, levallois core flaking and laminar flaking, as examples for learning (Figure 1-116 – Figure 1-126).

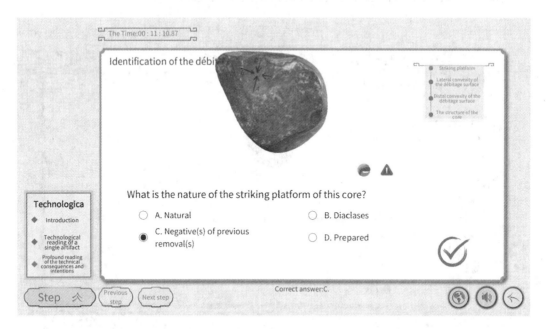

Figure 1-116　Choice Question About the Nature of the Striking Platform of the Core（1）

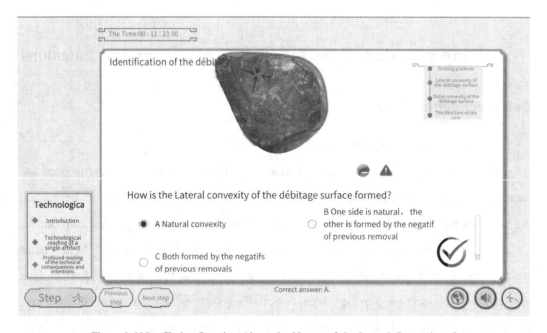

Figure 1-117　Choice Question About the Nature of the Lateral Convexity of

the *Débitage* Surface the Core（1）

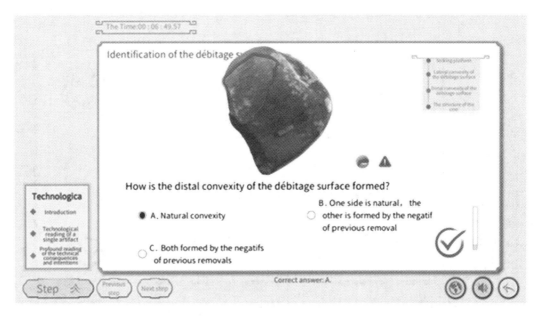

Figure 1-118   Choice Question About the Nature of the Distal Convexity of

the *Débitage* Surface of the Core（1）

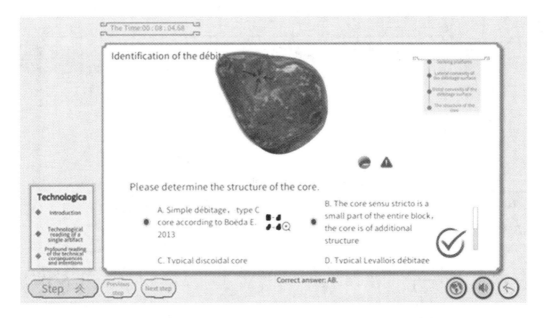

Figure 1-119   Choice Question About the Structure of the Core（1）

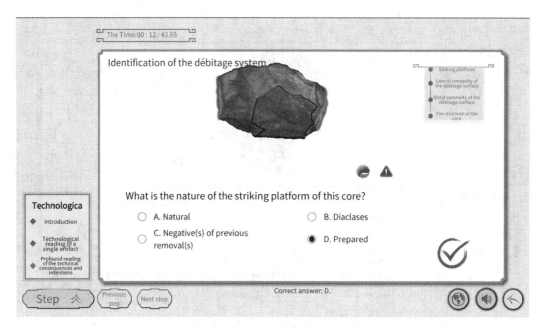

Figure 1-120 Choice Question About the Nature of the Striking Platform of the Core (2)

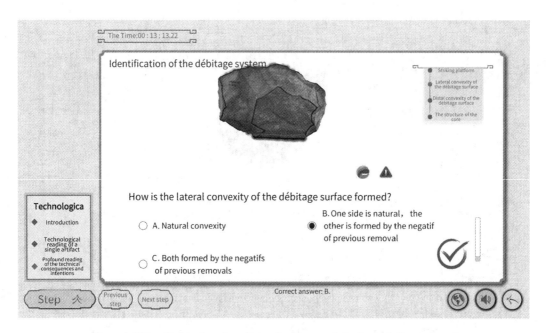

Figure 1-121 Choice Question About the Nature of the Lateral Convexity of

the *Débitage* Surface of the Core (2)

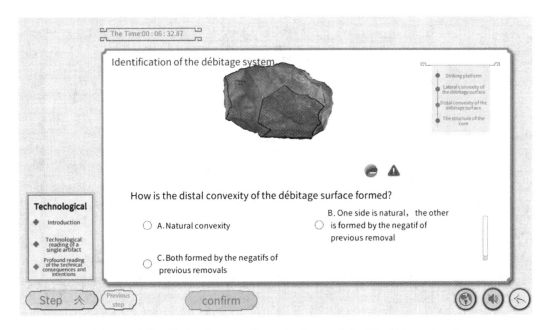

Figure 1-122   Choice Question About the Nature of the Distal Convexity of

the *Débitage* Surface of the Core（2）

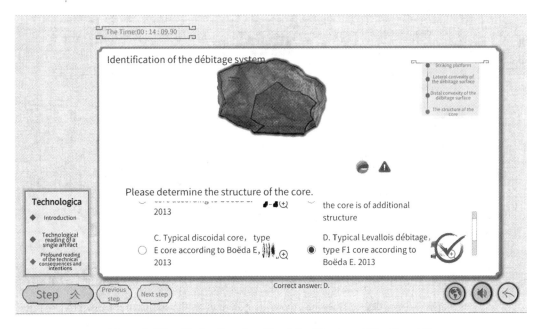

Figure 1-123   Choice Question About the Structure of the Core（2）

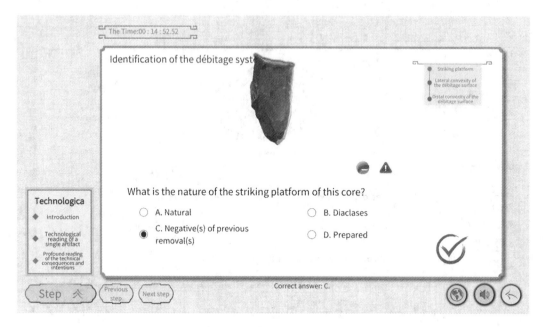

Figure 1-124   Choice Question About the Nature of the Striking Platform of the Core (3)

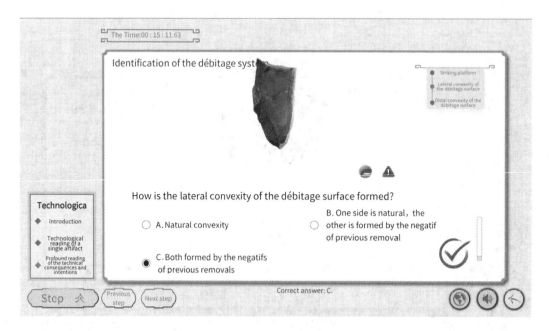

Figure 1-125   Choice Question About the Nature of the Lateral Convexity of

the *Débitage* Surface of the Core (3)

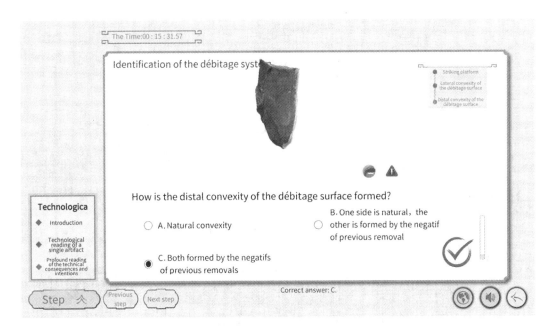

Figure 1-126   Choice Question About the Nature of the Distal Convexity of

the *Débitage* Surface of the Core（3）

（2）Techno-functional reading of shaped tools: Orientation.

Click "Next step" and enter the "Techno-functional reading of shaped tools" section. Students should first of all learn the layout and orientation conventions of shaped tools and use the mouse to rotate the specimen to its right position（Figure 1-127—Figure 1-128）.

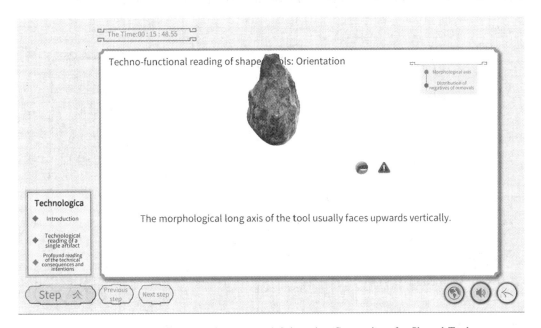

Figure 1-127   Interpretation of Layout and Orientation Conventions for Shaped Tools

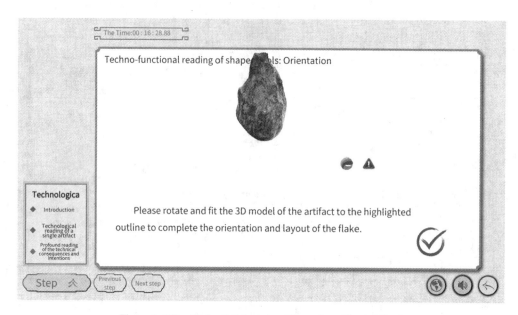

Figure 1-128　Task of Orientating Correctly a Shaped Tool

（3）Techno-functional reading of shaped tools: Metrical analysis.

Click "Next step" and enter the metrical analysis of shaped tools section. Use the ruler button of toolbars on the right to measure the length, width and thickness of the tool, and then fill the data in the blanks of the dialogue box. The system will check whether the data is correct. Based on the data, students will calculate the morphology type of the tool. We provide examples of bifacial and unifacial tools for learning and practicing (Figure 1-129).

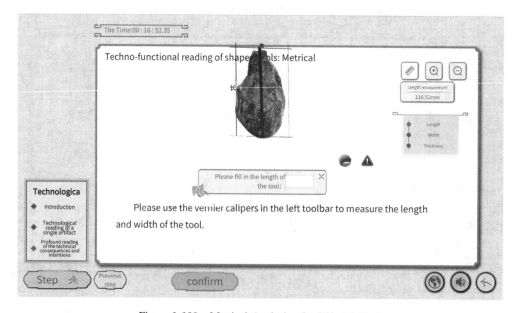

Figure 1-129　Metrical Analysis of a Bifacial Tool

Click "Next step" and complete the choice question (Figure 1-130–Figure 1-131).

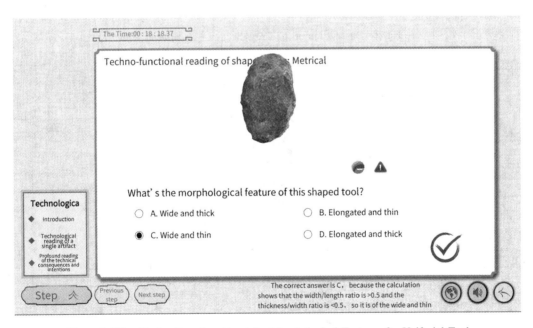

Figure 1-130　Choice Question About the Morphological Feature of a Bifacial Tool

Figure 1-131　Choice Question About the Morphological Feature of a Unifacial Tool

(4) Techno-functional reading of shaped tools: Observation of tool structure.

Click "Next step" and entre the section of "Observation of tool structure". Click on the tool in the right toolbar to truncate the stone tool model in any position and direction. Students can rotate the model at will to observe the cross-section pattern of the tool and answer the related questions. Two different bifaces are used for study (Figure 1-132—Figure 1-135).

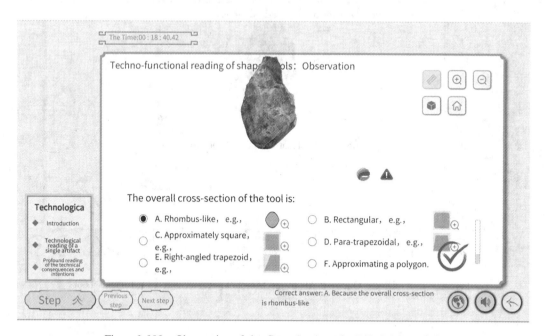

Figure 1-132    Observation of the Cross-Section of a Bifacial Tool (1)

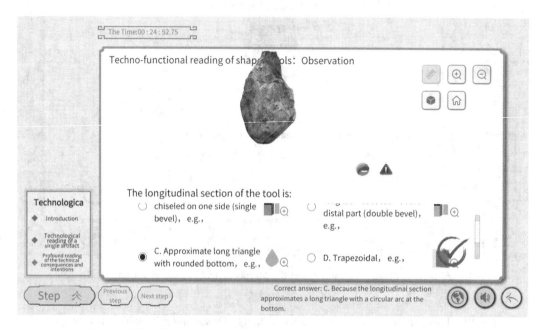

Figure 1-133    Observation of the Longitudinal Section of a Bifacial Tool (1)

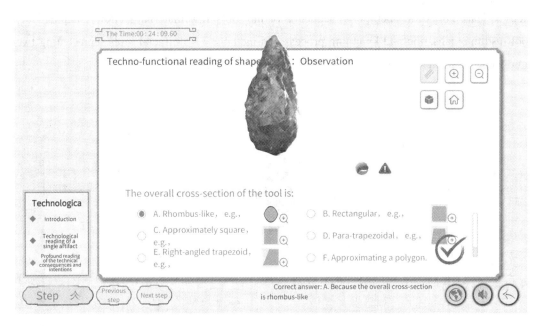

Figure 1-134　Observation of the Cross-Section of a Bifacial Tool（2）

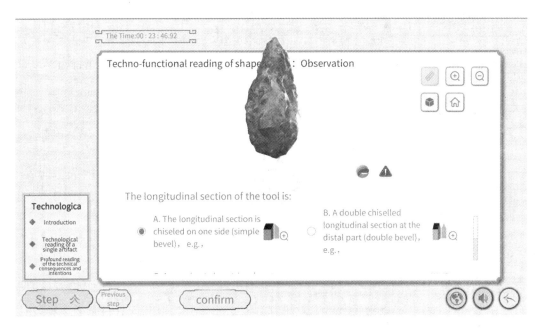

Figure 1-135　Observation of the Longitudinal Section of a Bifacial Tool（2）

（5）Techno-functional reading of shaped tools: Reconstruction of the operational sequence.

Click "Next step" and enter the section of "Reconstruction of the operational sequence of shaped tools". Students could rotate the 3D model to observe the artifact, and follow four steps to learn about the operational sequence of the tool: raw material section, shaping out, tool instrumentalisation and knapping process and method. Two bifacial tools representing two production strategies are provided in this part (Figure 1-136–Figure 1-143).

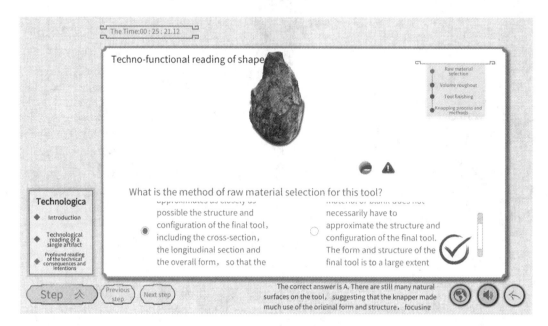

Figure 1-136    Choice Question About the Method of Raw Material Selection for the Tool (1)

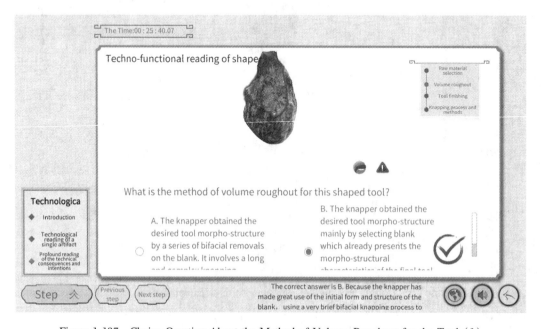

Figure 1-137    Choice Question About the Method of Volume Roughout for the Tool (1)

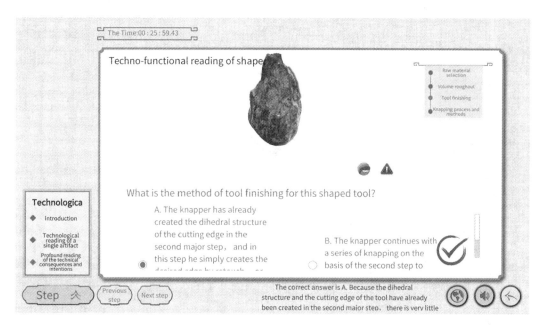

Figure 1-138　Choice Question About the Method of Tool Finishing for the Tool（1）

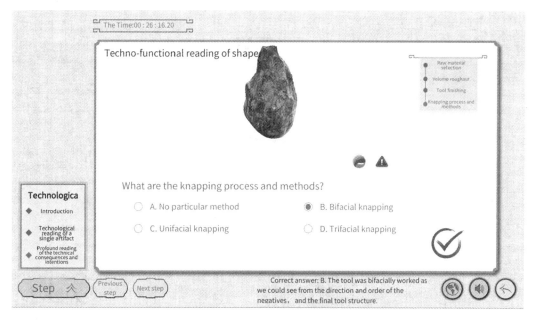

Figure 1-139　Choice Question About the Knapping Process and Methods for the Tool（1）

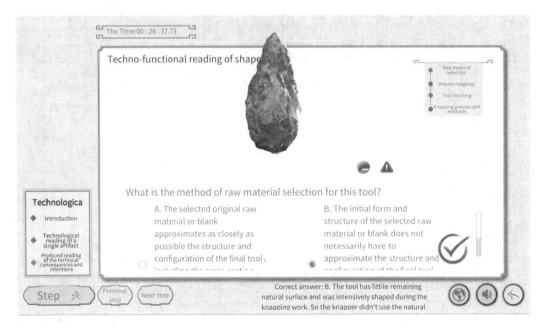

Figure 1-140   Choice Question About the Method of Raw Material Selection for the Tool (2)

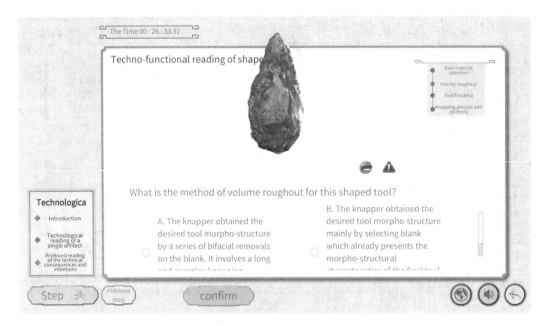

Figure 1-141   Choice Question About the Method of Volume Roughout for the Tool (2)

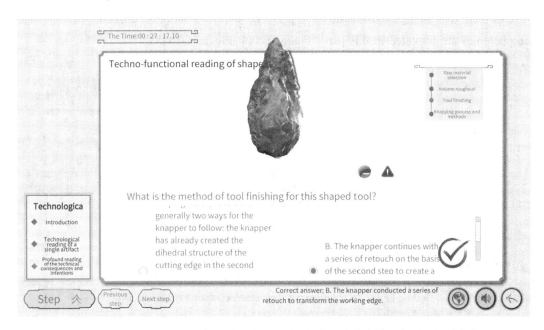

Figure 1-142　Choice Question About the Method of Tool Finishing for the Tool (2)

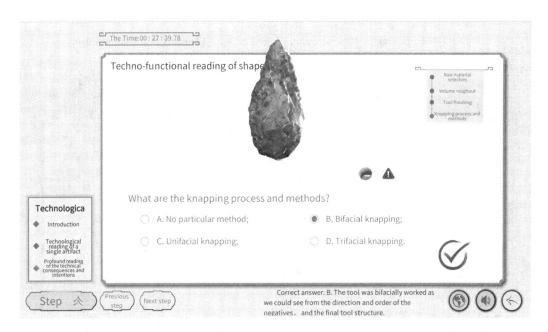

Figure 1-143　Choice Question About the Knapping Process and Methods for the Tool (2)

(6) Identification and presentation of the techno-functional units of the tool.

Click "Next step" and enter the section of "Identification and presentation of the techno-functional units of the tool", and learn the related theoretical knowledge. Then click "Next step" to observe the 3D specimen by rotating it. Identify the potential cutting edges and observe their morphologies from different perspectives. Two tools of different cutting edge morphologies are provided in this part (Figure 1-144—Figure 1-152).

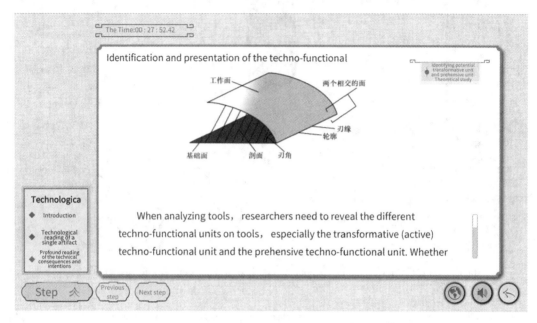

Figure 1-144    Schematic Representation of the Technical Elements of a Cutting Edge

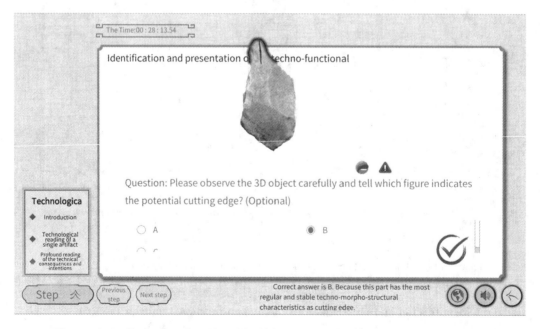

Figure 1-145    Choice Question About Identifying Potential Cutting Edge of a Bifacial Tool

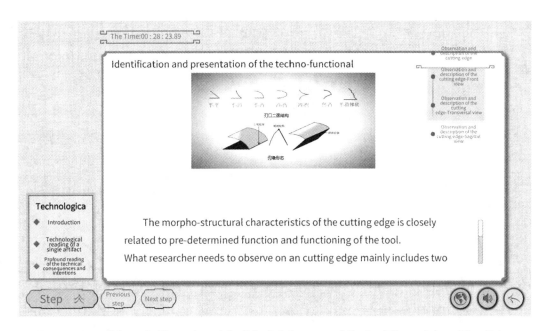

Figure 1-146　Schematic Illustration of the Dihedral Structure of Cutting Edge and three View Points for Describing a Cutting Edge

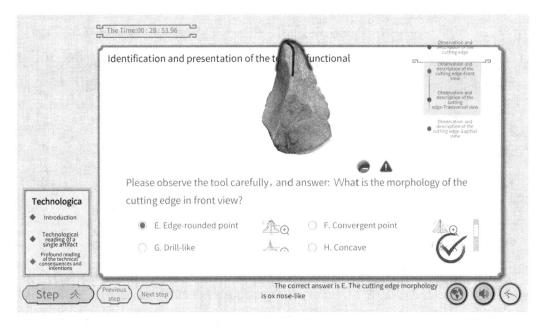

Figure 1-147　Choice Question About the Identification of the Cutting Edge Morphology in Front View of a Bifacial Tool（1）

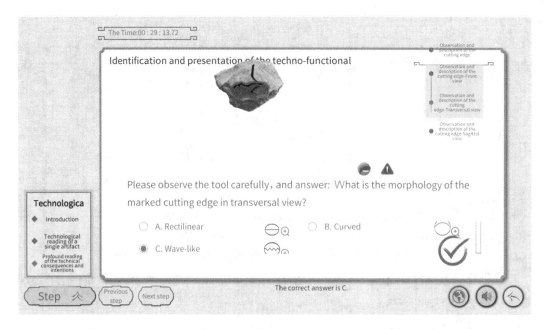

Figure 1-148   Choice Question About the Identification of the Cutting Edge Morphology in

Transversal View of a Bifacial Tool (1)

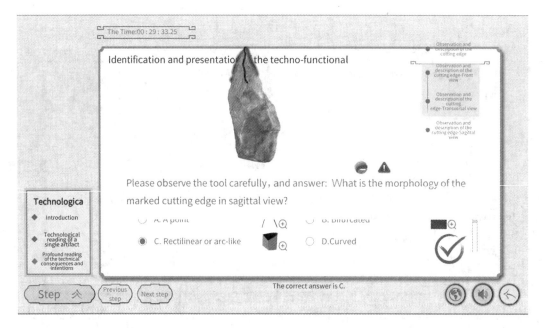

Figure 1-149   Choice Question About the Identification of the Cutting Edge Morphology in

Sagittal View of a Bifacial Tool (1)

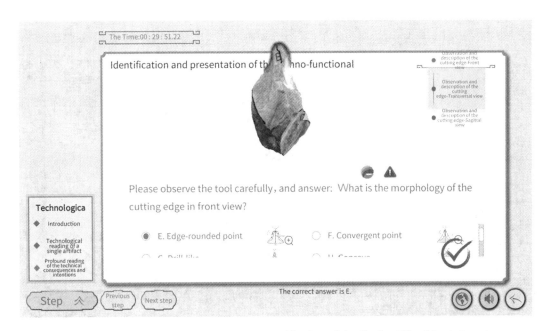

Figure 1-150　Choice Question About the Identification of the Cutting Edge Morphology in
Front View of a Bifacial Tool（2）

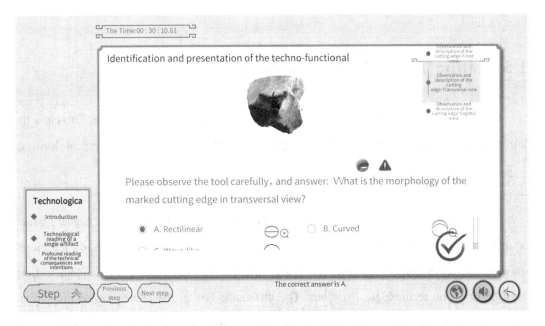

Figure 1-151　Choice Question About the Identification of the Cutting Edge Morphology in
Transversal View of a Bifacial Tool（2）

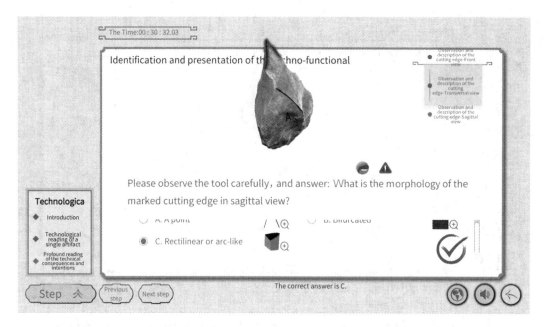

Figure 1-152    Choice Question About the Identification of the Cutting Edge Morphology in

Sagittal View of a Bifacial Tool (2)

## 1.5    Lithic Technological Drawing

Go back to the "Explore" module, and click "Lithic technological drawing" to enter the introduction and learn about the basic principles and methods of lithic technological drawing.

### 1.5.1    Introduction

Technological drawing is a skill that researchers of lithic technology must master, which is an illustration of the result of technological reading. Two styles are often used: traditional drawing and technological drawing. They are different but still related to each other. Both must be based on technological reading. The difference lies in the expression of the surface condition. Traditional drawing focuses on the shade of scars and three-dimensional effect, while technological drawing does not present the shade of scars, but uses conventional symbols, such as numbers, letters, colors, etc., to indicate the surface condition, scar direction, chronology and number, as well as the structural and techno-functional characteristics of the tools with working edges. Technological drawing is also an international langue in lithic studies. In this module, we will study how to draw a flake, a core and a shaped tool as well as the major rules and points for drawing (Figure 1-153).

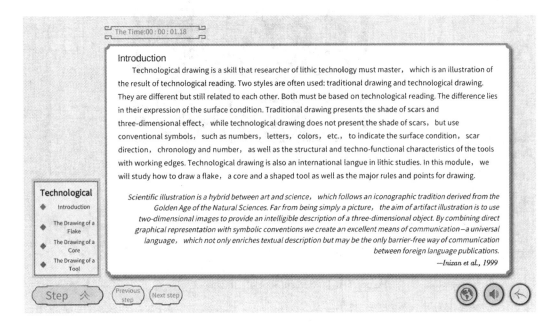

Figure 1-153　Interpretation of the Significance of Lithic Technological Drawing

## 1.5.2　Drawing of a Flake

The Drawing of a Flake

◎ **Experimental Steps**:

Click "Next step" to enter the section of "Drawing of a Flake". By controlling the video progress button, watch the teaching video about drawing a flake before answering the corresponding questions.

(1) When preparing drawing tools, please pay attention to the drawing tool types in the video (Figure 1-154).

(2) Based on previously learnt knowledge, observe the flake and pose it in the right position (Figure 1-155).

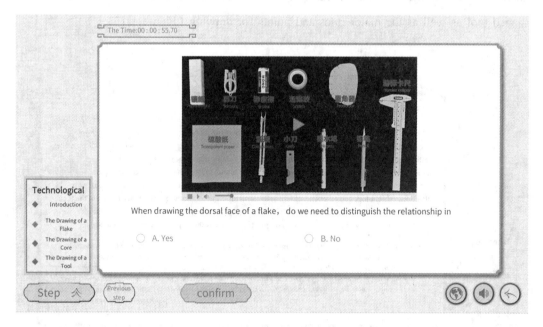

Figure 1-154　Screen Shot of Drawing Tools

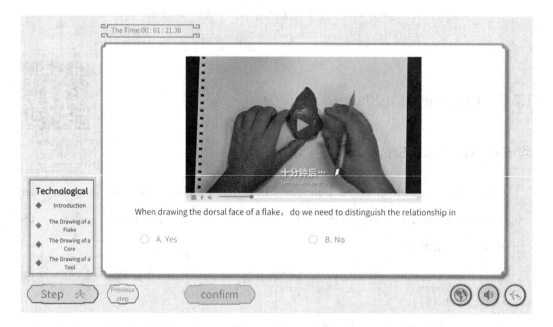

Figure 1-155　Screen Shot of Flake Positioning Before Drawing

（3）Draw the contour of the flake after correctly posing it on the drawing paper（Figure 1-156）.

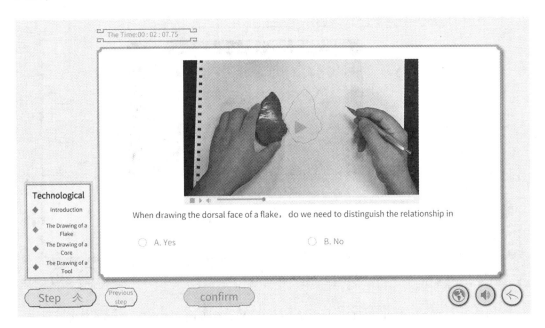

Figure 1-156　Draw the Flake's Contour

（4）Draw the scars（Figure 1-157）.

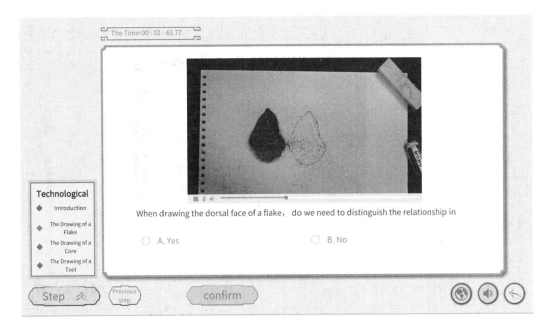

Figure 1-157　Draw the Scars

（5）Draw the profile, ventral face and butt (Figure 1-158).

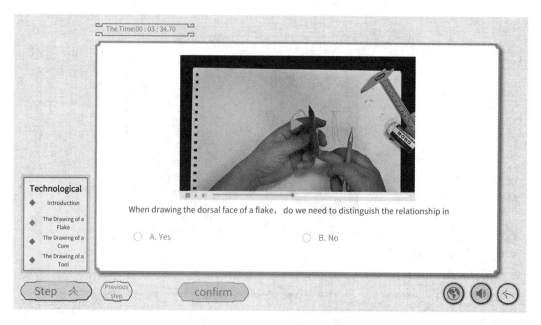

Figure 1-158　Draw the Profile, Ventral Face and Butt With the Help of a Vernier Caliper

（6）Identify and note the knapping order and direction of previous negatives (Figure 1-159).

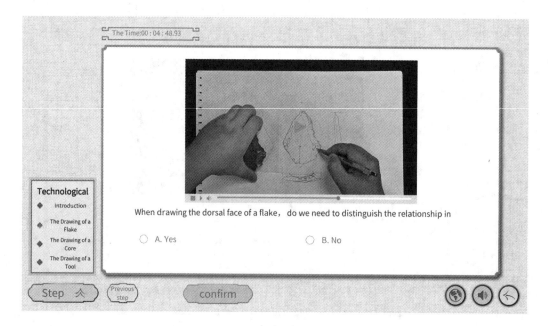

Figure 1-159　Note the Knapping Order and Direction of Previous Negatives

(7) Make a copy with the transparent paper and scan it (Figure 1-160).

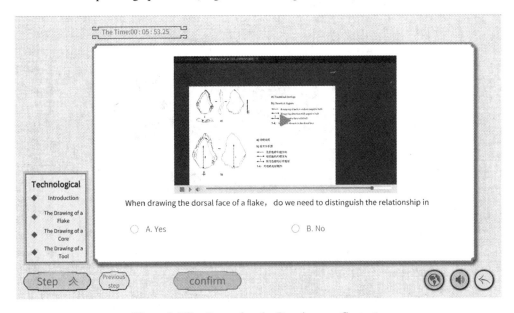

When drawing the dorsal face of a flake, do we need to distinguish the relationship in

A. Yes    B. No

Figure 1-160　Make a Copy with the Transparent Paper and Scan it

(8) Process drawings with computer software. Whilst keeping the traditional drawing, complete the technical drawing of the artifact by labelling the direction of knapping of the flake with arrows, labelling the order of previous scars with numbers, and noting the meaning of the relevant technical symbols on the side. Summarize the main points of the drawing and answer the corresponding question (Figure 1-161−Figure 1-162).

When drawing the dorsal face of a flake, do we need to distinguish the relationship in

A. Yes    B. No

Figure 1-161　Processing the Drawings on Computer

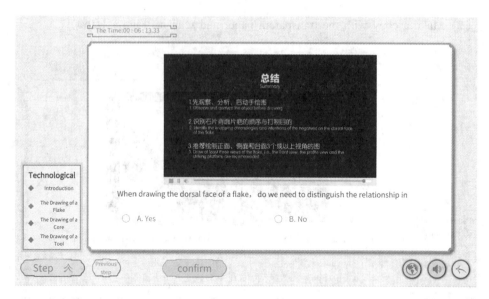

Figure 1-162    Summary of the Drawing of a Flake

## 1.5.3   Drawing of a Core

The Drawing of
a Core

◎ **Experimental Steps**：

Click "Next step" and enter the section of "Drawing of a core". By controlling the video progress button, watch the teaching video about drawing a core before answering the corresponding questions.

（1）Prepare drawing tools（Figure 1-163）.

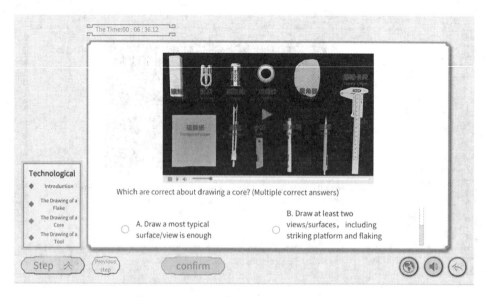

Figure 1-163    Screen Shot of Drawing Tools

（2）Observe and orient the core correctly based on the knowledge that we have learnt before（Figure 1-164）.

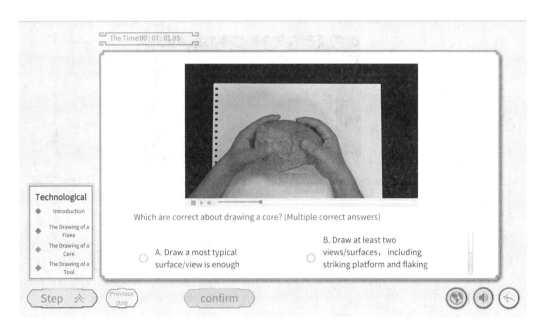

Figure 1-164 Observe and Orient the Core

（3）Draw the contour, flaking surface, striking platform and note the reduction order of the scars（Figure 1-165）.

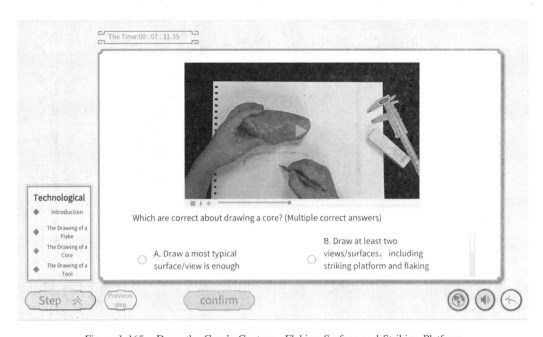

Figure 1-165 Draw the Core's Contour, Flaking Surface and Striking Platform

（4）Use transparent paper to make a copy of the drawing and scan it（Figure 1-166）.

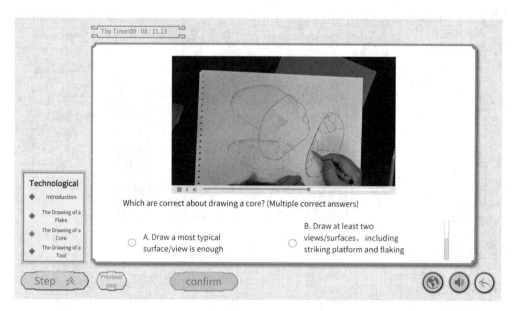

Figure 1-166　Use Transparent Paper to Make a Copy of the Drawing and Scan it

（5）Process drawings with computer software. Interpret the knapping order, knapping direction of each scar and technical consequence of each negative on the core. And add some remarks on the relevant technical symbols on the side. Summarize the main points of the drawing and answer the corresponding question（Figure 1-167-Figure 1-168）.

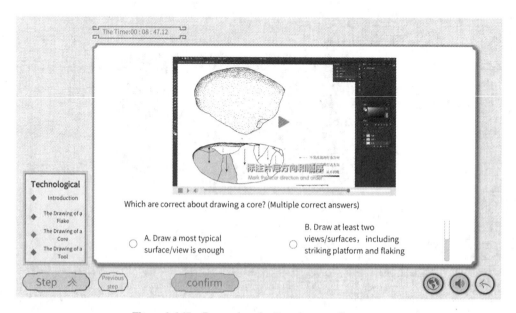

Figure 1-167　Processing the Drawings on Computer

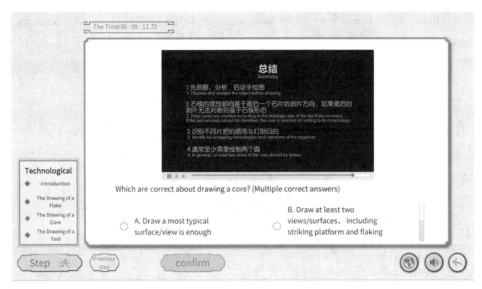

Figure 1-168　Summary of the Drawing of a Core

## 1.5.4　Drawing of a Shaped Tool

### ◎ **Experimental Steps：**

The Drawing of a Shaped Tool

Click "Next step" and enter the section of "Drawing of a shaped tool".
By controlling the video progress button, watch the teaching video about
drawing a shaped tool and answer the corresponding questions.

（1）Prepare drawing tools（Figure 1-169）.

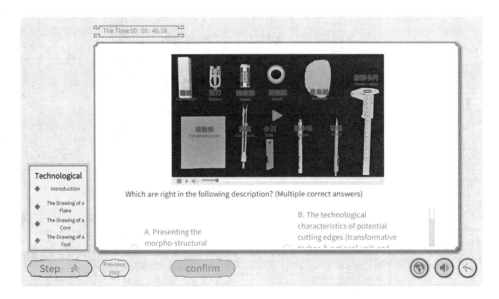

Figure 1-169　Prepare Drawing Tools

（2）Observe and orient the shaped tool correctly based on the knowledge that we have learnt before（Figure 1-170）.

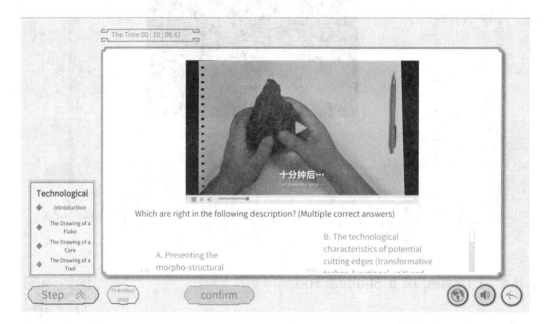

Figure 1-170    Observe and Orient the Shaped Tool Before Drawing

（3）The specimen is a biface; draw its contour and scars（Figure 1-171）.

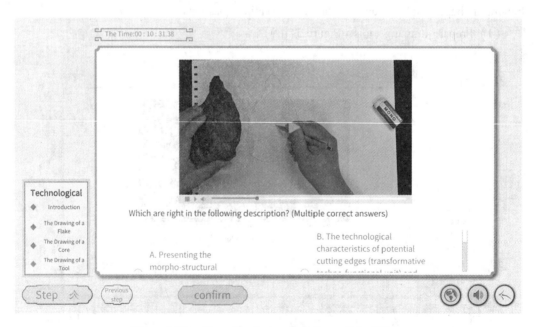

Figure 1-171    Draw the Contour and Scars of the Biface

(4) Draw the profile (Figure 1-172).

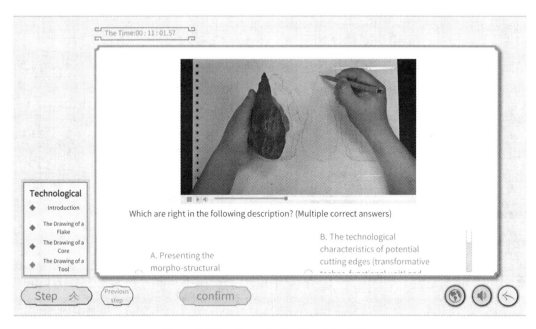

Figure 1-172   Draw the Profile of the Biface

(5) Draw the cross-sections of the biface (Figure 1-173).

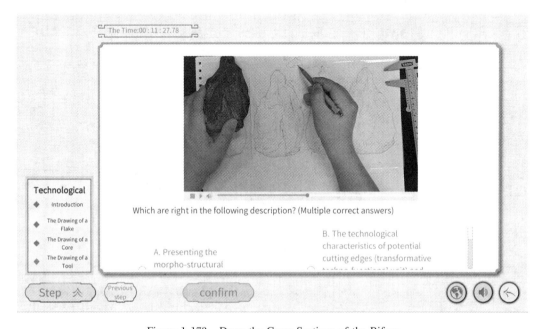

Figure 1-173   Draw the Cross-Sections of the Biface

（6）According to previous knowledge, please identify the techno-functional units of the tool（Figure 1-174）.

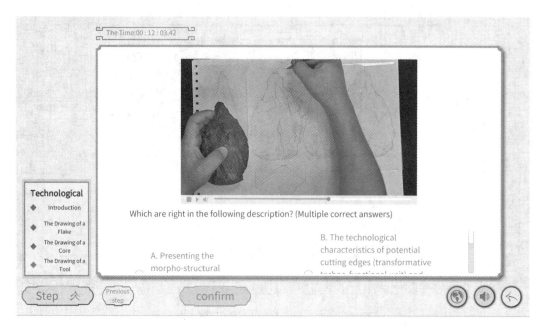

Figure 1-174  Identify and Note the Technical Data of Different Techno-functional Units

（7）Make a copy of the drawing with transparent paper and scan it（Figure 1-175）.

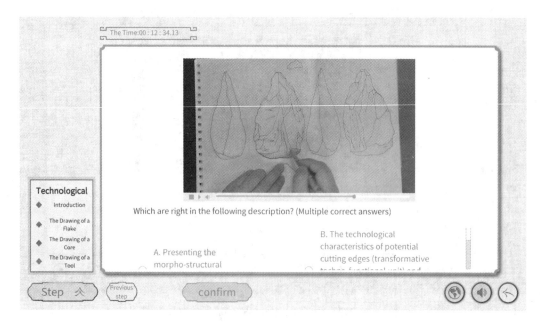

Figure 1-175  Make a Copy of the Drawing with Transparent Paper and Scan it

（8）Use computer software to process the drawings. Complete the technical drawings of the techno-productional and techno-functional analysis results. And add some remarks on the symbols used at the side. Summarize the main points of the drawing and answer the corresponding question（Figure 1-176-Figure 1-177）.

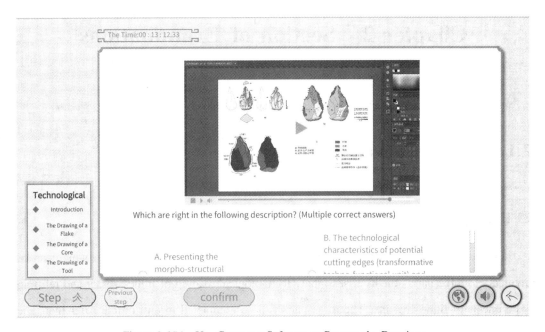

Figure 1-176　Use Computer Software to Process the Drawings

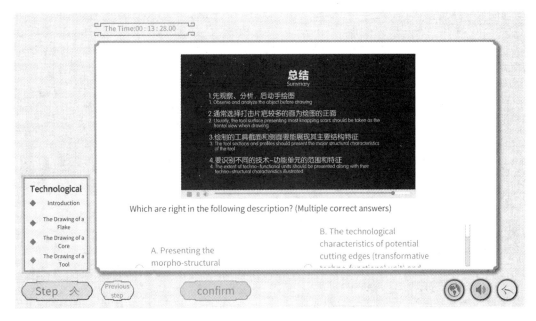

Figure 1-177　Summary of the Drawing of a Shaped Tool

# Chapter 2   Section of Examinations

## 2.1   Theory Assessment

### ◎ Experimental Steps:

Go back to the main menu of the site and click "Section of examinations", which can be divided into three parts: theory assessment, technological reading of lithic artifact and refitting experiments of lithic artifacts. The three parts can be completed in any order. After that, the score will appear on the screen, and constitute a part of the final score (Figure 2-1).

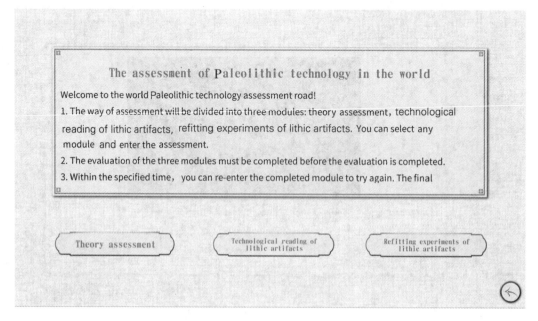

Figure 2-1   Interface of the Section of Examinations

Click "Next step" and complete the questions in turn (Figure 2-2).

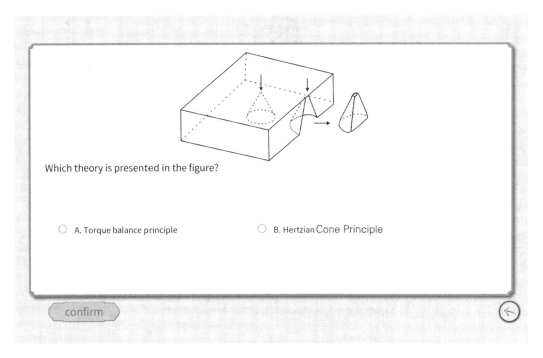

Which theory is presented in the figure?

○  A. Torque balance principle          ○  B. Hertzian Cone Principle

confirm

Figure 2-2   Theoretical Test About the Hertzian Cone Principle

## 2.2   Test About Lithic Technological Reading

### ◎ Experimental Steps:

Go back to the module of "Section of Examinations" and click the section of "technological reading of artifacts" before answering the questions in turn (Figure 2-3).

## 2.3   Test About the Refitting Experiments

### ◎ Experimental Steps:

Go back to the module of "section of examinations" and click the section "refitting experiments of lithic artifacts". Complete the refitting according to the given hints (Figure 2-4).

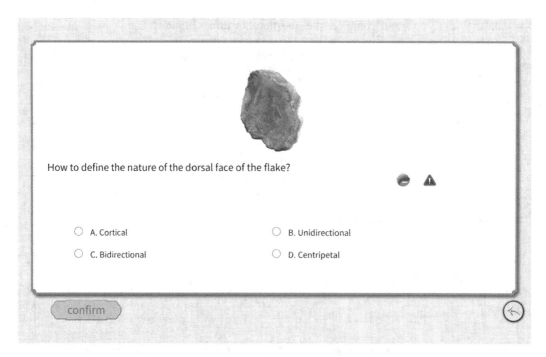

Figure 2-3   Test About the Technological Reading

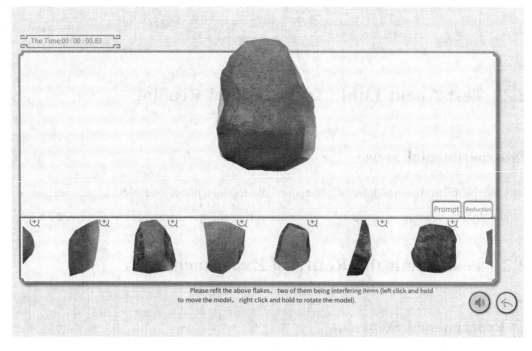

Figure 2-4   Test of Lithic Refitting

# Chapter 3   Experimental Platform Operation and Technical Explanations

## 3.1   Instructions for Logging into the Virtual Simulation Experiment Platform

(1) On-campus personnel: use the student account and password to enter the virtual simulation platform of Wuhan University.

(2) Off-campus personnel: enter the experimental platform through real-name authentication.

(3) After entering the experimental platform, you can see modules such as "Experimental Principles", "Journey of Discovery", "Section of Examinations", "References", and "Experimental Results". Click to see the corresponding content.

(4) After completing the "Section of Examinations" module, click on the "Experimental Results", and you can view and upload the student's score.

## 3.2   Special Technical Operating Instructions When Using the Platform

(1) Click on any module to start exploring without having to learn it sequentially from beginning to end.

(2) By clicking on the symbol ⚠ next to the specimen photo or 3D model, you can get information about the origin, age and other important information of the artifact.

(3) Method of rotating all specimen 3D models: Hold down the right mouse button to grab the 3D model to rotate the specimen.

(4) All 3D models of lithic specimens are available in high resolution. Please click on

this icon ⬤ to view the "Cloud Earth" 3D model of the specimen in high resolution.

(5) The progress of each module cannot be saved on the web, so please complete each module at once.

## 3.3   Description of "Cloud Earth" Hyperlinks

(1) Click on the circular "Cloud Earth" icon ⬤ to jump to the corresponding specimen's hyperlink.

(2) Hold down the left or right mouse button to drag and rotate the specimen to observe the specimen from different viewpoints; you can also use the mouse wheel to zoom in and out of the 3D model in order to observe the specimen details (Figure 3-1).

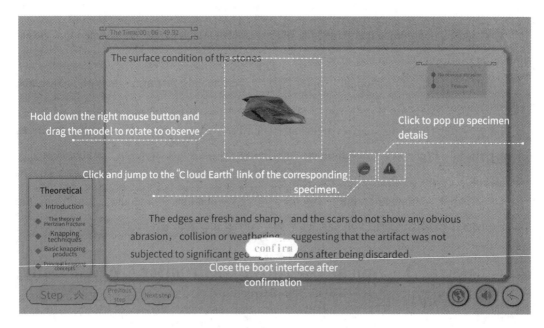

Figure 3-1   Explanations for Operation with a Mouse

## 3.4   Other Remarks

(1) On the left side of the interface is a menu of steps and a progress indicator bar, with small steps that can be jumped to at will.

（2）Steps in progress are shown in orange, and completed or uncompleted steps are in grey.

（3）Once you enter the "Journey of Exploration", each completed module will show completed in the "Journey of Exploration" interface.

# Summary of Explanations of Terminology

**The theory of Hertzian fracture**: A Hertzian cone is a cone created when an object passes through a solid, such as a bullet through glass. Strictly speaking, it is a cone of force formed when passing through a brittle, amorphous or cryptocrystalline solid material from the point of impact. This force eventually creates a complete or incomplete cone in the raw material. This physical principle explains the morphology and characteristics of flakes during lithic production.

**Knapping techniques**: A technique being the practical manner of accomplishing a particular task. We define a "technique" as one of the procedures in manufacturing a craft (and sometimes an art), e.g., lithic artifacts of the prehistoric knapper. Examples of techniques are: direct percussion with a hammerstone, the *débitage* of a blade by pressure-flaking, and the fracture of a bladelet by means of the microburin blow (Inizan et al., 1999, pp. 156-157). Common techniques include freehand technique, anvil technique, bipolar-on-anvil technique, throwing technique, and pressure technique. Technique corresponds to the lower-most level of knowledge in the lithic technological system.

**Freehand technique**: Freehand technique is the process of using a hammer and concentrating on a point on the surface of the stone near the edge to crack the stone with the help of the Hertzian cone principle. It can be used to process both flake blanks and tools. Depending on the presence or absence of an intermediary between the hammer and the raw material, this technique can be divided into two manners: direct and indirect knapping.

**Anvil technique**: Anvil technique is the process of knapping a stone on another passive stone, the anvil, in order to crack it. This technique is more common in China compared to other regions of the world.

**Bipolar-on-anvil technique**: Bipolar-on-anvil technique is the process of placing the stone on an anvil and using a hammer to fracture the stone at the right angle and with the right force.

**Throwing technique**: Throwing technique is the process of using a standing position and throwing the stone in your hand onto the anvil, thus fracturing the raw material.

**Pressure technique**: Unlike percussion, this technique of fracturing hard stone is carried out with a tool whose extremity applies pressure to detach a flake. Pressure can be used for *débitage* or retouching.

**Cobble**: The raw material selected by hominins for making stone tools is usually a natural rock with a smooth surface and no sharp edges, also known as river gravels. They are transported by water and more or less weathered after being deposited on the river bank. The surface roundness of these gravels varies from the distance and kinetic energy of water flow. The pebbles on river banks are usually transported away from their primary veins and are secondary buried. Geologically they are further classified as fine, coarse and massive gravels depending on their size. In Palaeolithic research, gravels are generally divided into small (pebble, <70 mm), large (cobble, ≥70 mm) and giant (boulder, ≥25 cm).

**Vein nodules**: Vein nodules are raw materials exploited by hominins in mountainous rock-strip accumulations for use in the making of stone tools. Geologically, they are mineral aggregates that differ significantly from the surrounding rock in terms of composition, structure and colour and have a clear interface with the surrounding rock. They are often developed in the rock formations of mountain ranges. What was mined by the ancient humans were usually relatively homogeneous, isotropic clasts or nodules exposed and spalled from these mineral assemblages by weathering or other causes. They have not been transported by water or wind and are buried *in situ*.

**Limestone breccia**: Limestone caves or rock shelters often contain blocks that have been spalled down by weathering and other causes, the main mineral compositions being carbonate and calcite, which are slightly softer than flint. The sharpness of the surface varies according to the degree of weathering or water rounding, and some have calcareous cements attached to the surface. Hominins used to select suitable limestone blocks for making stone tools.

**Flake**: A general term for a fragment that is removed from a hard stone: either from a core or from a cobble or a tool, etc. As a result of the Hertzian fracture, flakes have similar recognizable features, including butt/striking platform, point of impact, bulb, waves/ripples, dorsal face, ventral face, flaking angle, flaking direction, hackles.

**Core**: The cores are generally the remaining volumes after flaking. As a result of the

Hertzian fracture principle, the surface of the core produces a number of recognizable features, including striking platform, impact point, counter-bulb, arrises, platform angle, surface of *débitage*, knapping direction, hackles, waves/ripples, etc. Theoretically, the core and the flake are originally from one volume. The difference between the two is that the flake generally has a prominent bulb below the butt, while the corresponding location on the core is a depression, i.e., a counter-bulb.

**The concept of production**: The concept of production refers to the way in which the blank or tool is manufactured. Theoretically, there are two major production concepts in the Palaeolithic technology, namely *débitage* and shaping.

**Débitage**: It is a term conventionally used to denote the intentional knapping of blocks (raw material), in order to obtain products that will either be subsequently shaped or retouched, or directly used without further modification (Inizan et al., 1999).

**Surface of *débitage***: it is the surface from which the flakes are removed. The dorsal face of a flake corresponds to the surface of *débitage*.

**Shaping**: Shaping is a knapping operation carried out for the purpose of manufacturing a single artifact by sculpting the raw material in accordance with the desired form. In archaeology, the term applies to the manufacture of bifacial, trihedral, polyhedral pieces, etc., whatever the nature of the blank and the size of the finished product are. Shaping generally involves two successive phases, roughing out and finishing, and can bring into play a number of techniques. Unlike *débitage*, the purpose of the operation is not to obtain blanks—although shaping often produces a high number of flakes—but to transform any type of blank into a tool (Inizan et al., 1999).

**Refitting (Conjoining)**: It involves matching pieces or fragments after having identified their positive and negative knapping surfaces (*débitage*, retouch), or their fracture surfaces, and then fitting them together and verifying that they are in fact complementary. It helps not only to reconstruct the knapping process and sequences and the site structure and taphonomic process but also to understand the spacial organization of hominins.

**Technological reading of lithic artifacts**: It is necessary to go through the process of technological reading a stone object before attempting to study the lithic assemblage it belongs to. The reading of an object brings into play the raw material used, as well as the technical actions and the knowledge, which together work towards the conception of the tool, in the broader sense of the term (tool, weapon, tool component...). It takes place on two levels:

the first level is that of observation, an initial reading of knapping scars, and the second level is one of inference. This is the matter of interpreting the interdependence of artifacts in the *chaîne opératoire*, even if links are missing.

**Techno-functional unit**: According to the principle of "cutting edge first", techno-functional unit is defined as "a series of technical elements or characters integrated as an entity through synergy". One tool *sensu stricto* must be constituted by two techno-functional units; one is transformative techno-functional unit on which cutting edge is located, the other is prehensive techno-functional unit. Between them there exists a part that transmits energy, but to be simple, this part is usually not considered during study. So a tool is usually deconstructed into two units: transformative techno-functional unit and prehensive techno-functional unit.

**Technological drawing of lithic artifacts**: Traditional drawing presents the shade of scars and the three-dimensional effect of the artifact, while technological drawing does not present the shade of scars, but uses conventional symbols, such as numbers, letters, colors, etc., to indicate the surface condition, scar direction, chronology and number, as well as the structural and techno-functional characteristics of the tools with working edges. Technological drawing is also an international langue in lithic studies.

# 参 考 文 献

## （1）西文文献

［1］Audouze F. (1999). New advances in French prehistory. Antiquity, 73(3), 167-175.

［2］Audouze F., & Karlin C. (2017). La chaîne opératoire a 70 ans：qu'en ont fait les préhistoriens français. Journal of Lithic Studies, 4(2), 5-73.

［3］Belyaeva E. V., & Shchelinsky V. E. (2022). The birth of the Acheulian techno-complex in the Caucasus region. L'Anthropologie, 126(1), 102973.

［4］Beshkani A. (2018). Analyse Techno-Fonctionnelle des Industries Lithiques Mousté-riennes des sites du Zagros：Les Grottes de Bisitun, Shanidar et l'Abri Warwasi. PhD thesis. Paris.

［5］Boëda E. (1986). Approche technologique du concept Levallois et évaluation de son champ d'application à travers trois gisements saaliens et weichseliens de la France septentrionale. PhD thesis. Paris：Université de Paris X-Nanterre.

［6］Boëda E. (1988). Le concept laminaire：rupture et filiation avec le concept Levallois, in L'Homme de Neandertal. Vol. 8. La Mutation.

［7］Boëda E. (1989). La conception trifaciale d'un nouveau mode de taille Paléolithique, Les premiers peuplements humains de l'Europe, 114° Congr. nat. Soc. sav., Paris, pp. 251-263.

［8］Boëda E., Geneste J., & Meignen L. (1990). Identification de chaînes opératoires lithiques du Paléolithique ancien et moyen. Paléo, 2(1), 43-80.

［9］Boëda E. (1990). De la surface au volume analyse des conceptions des *débitage*s levallois et laminaire. Paper presented at Paléolithique moyen récent et Paléolithique supérieur ancien en Europe. Colloque international de Nemours, 9-11 mai 1988. Mémoires du Musée de Préhist. d'Ile-de-France,3,1990. pp. 63-68.

[10] Boëda E. (1991). Approche de la variabilité des systèmes de production lithique des industries du Paléolithique inférieur et moyen: chronique d'une variabilité attendue. Techniques et culture, (17-18), 37-79.

[11] Boëda E. (1993). Le *débitage* Discoïde et le *débitage* Levallois récurrent centripète. Bulletin de la Société Préhistorique Française, 90(6), 392-404.

[12] Boëda E. (1994). Le concept Levallois: variabilité des méthodes. Paris: Editions du CNRS. Monographies du CRA 19.

[13] Boëda E. (1995). Levallois: a volumetric construction, methods, a technique. In: D. Harold L. & O. Bar-Yosef (Eds.), The Definition and Interpretation of Levallois Technology (pp. 41-65). Madison: Prehistory Press.

[14] Boëda E. (1997). Technogenèse de systèmes de production lithique au Paléolithique inférieur et moyen en Europe occidentale et au Proche-Orient: Université de Paris X—Nanterre, Habilitation à diriger des recherches, 2 vol., Nanterre.

[15] Boëda E. (1999). A Levallois point embedded in the vertebra of a wild ass (Equus africanus): hafting, projectiles and Mousterian hunting weapons. Antiquity, 73(280), 394-402.

[16] Boëda E. (2001). Détermination des unités techno-fonctionnelles de pièces bifaciales provenant de la couche acheuléenne C'3 base du site de Barbas I. In: D. D. Cliquet (Ed.), Les industries à outils bifaciaux du Paléolithique moyen d'Europe occidentale (pp. 51-75): Actes de la Table-ronde Internationale Organisée à Caen (Basse-Normandie, France), 14-15 Octobre 1999.

[17] Boëda E. (2004). Relationship between East and West Asia in Paleolithic age. Quaternary Sciences, 24(3), 255-264.

[18] Boëda E. (2005). Paléo-technologie ou anthropologie des techniques. Arobase, 1, 46-64.

[19] Bodin É. (2011). Analyse techno-fonctionnelle des industries à pièces bifaciales aux pléistocènes inférieur et moyen en Chine. PhD thesis. Pékin: Université Paris Ouest Nanterre La Défense et Institut de Paléontologie des Vertébrés et de Paléoanthrophologie (Académie des Sciences de Chine).

[20] Boëda E. (2013). Techno-logique & Technologie: une Paléo-histoire des objets lithiques tranchants. France: @rchéo-éditions. com.

[21] Boëda E. (2014). Le Concept Levallois: variabilité des méthodes. France: @rchéo-

éditions. com.

[22] Boëda E., Rocca R., Da Costa A., Fontugne M., Hatté C., & Clemente-Conte I. (2016). New Data on a Pleistocene Archaeological Sequence in South America: Toca do Sítio do Meio, Piauí, Brazil. Paleo America, 2(4), 286-302.

[23] Boëda E., & Ramos M. P. (2017). The affordance: a conceptual tool for a better understanding of the tools. Paper presented at the 11th International symposium on knappable materials "From toolstone to stone tools". Necochea.

[24] Boëda E. (2019). Intégrer le temps long pour mieux appréhender le changement technique en Préhistoire. In É. David (Ed.), Anthropologie des techniques. Cahier 1. De la mémoire aux gestes en Préhistoire (pp. 63-76). Paris: Éditions l'Harmattan.

[25] Boëda E. (2021). Le Phénomène technique en préhistoire une réflexion épistémologique à partir et autour du Levallois. Paris: l'Harmattan.

[26] Boëda E., Ramos M., Pérez A., Hatté C., Lahaye C., & Pino M. (2021). 24. 0 kyr cal BP stone artifact from Vale da Pedra Furada, Piauí, Brazil: Techno-functional analysis. PLoS One, 16(3), e247965.

[27] Bonilauri S. (2010). Les outils du Paléolithique moyen : une mémoire technique oubliée? Approche techno-fonctionnelle appliquée à un assemblage lithique de conception Levallois provenant du site d'Umm el Tlel (Syrie centrale). Doctoral thesis. Paris: Université Paris Ouest Nanterre La Défense.

[28] Carbonell E., Bermúdez De Castro J. M., Parés J. M., Pérez-González A., Cuenca-Bescós G., & Ollé A. (2008). The first hominin of Europe. Nature, 452(7186), 465-469.

[29] Carr A. P. (1982). Cobble. In: M. Schwartz (Ed.), Beaches and Coastal Geology (p. 328). Boston, MA: Springer US.

[30] Chevrier B. (2006). De l'Acheuléen méridional au technocomplexe trifacial : la face cachée des industries du Bergeracois. Apport de l'analyse technologique de l'industrie lithique de Barbas I C'4 sup (Creysse, Dordogne). Gallia Préhistoire, (48), 207-252.

[31] Chevrier B. (2012). Les assemblages à pièces bifaciales au Pléistocène inférieur et moyen ancien en Afrique de l'Est et au Proche—Orient: Nouvelle approche du phénomène bifacial appliquée aux problématiques de migrations, de diffusion et d'évolution locale. PhD thesis. Paris: Université Paris Ouest Nanterre La Défense.

[32] Clarkson C., Jacobs Z., Marwick B., Fullagar R., Wallis L., & Smith M. (2017).

Human occupation of northern Australia by 65,000 years ago. Nature, 547(7663), 306-310.

[33]Clark G. (1969). World prehistory: a new outline. Cambridge: Cambridge University Press.

[34]Dambricourt Malassé A., Moigne A., Singh M., Calligaro T., Karir B., & Gaillard C. (2016). Intentional cut marks on bovid from the Quranwala zone, 2.6 Ma, Siwalik Frontal Range, northwestern India. Comptes Rendus Palevol, 15(3-4), 317-339.

[35]Dambricourt Malassé A. (2016). The first Indo-French Prehistorical Mission in Siwaliks and the discovery of anthropic activities at 2. 6 million years. Comptes Rendus Palevol, 15(3-4), 281-294.

[36]Dauvois M., (1976) Précis de dessin dynamique et structural des industries lithiques préhistoriques. Périgueux : Fanlac, 264p, ill.

[37]David É. (Ed. ) (2019). Anthropologie des techniques. Cahier 1. De la mémoire aux gestes en Préhistoire. Paris: Éditions l'Harmattan.

[38]De Weyer L. (2020). Les premières traditions techniques du Paléolithique ancien. Paris: L'Harmattan.

[39]De Weyer L., Pérez A., Hoguin R., Forestier H., & Boëda E. (2022). Time, memory and alterity in prehistoric lithic technology: Synthesis and perspectives of the French technogenetic approach. Journal of Lithic Studies, 9(1).

[40]Forestier H. (1993). Le Clactonien: mise en application d'une nouvelle méthode de *débitage* s'inscrivant dans la variabilité des systèmes de production lithique du Paléolithique ancien. Paléo, Revue d'Archéologie Préhistorique, 5, 53-82.

[41]Forestier H. (2020). La pierre et son ombre: Epistémologie de la préhistoire. Paris: Éditions l'Harmattan.

[42]Forestier H., & Boëda E. (2018). Outil préhistorique. In: A. Raulin, I. Rivoal, A. Piette & J. Salankis (Eds. ), Dictionnaire de l'humain (pp. 401-409). Paris: Presses universitaires de Paris Ouest.

[43]Gao X., & Norton C. J. (2002). A critique of the Chinese "Middle Palaeolithic". Antiquity, 76, 397-412.

[44]Goebel T., Waters M. R., & O'Rourke D. H. (2008). The Late Pleistocene Dispersal of Modern Humans in the Americas. Science, 319(5869), 1497-1502.

[45]Guidon N., & Delibrias G. (1986). Carbon-14 dates point to man in the Americas

32,000 years ago. Nature,（321）, 769-771.

[46] Gowlett J. A. J. （1993）. How to Skin an Elephant, Nature, 362, 672.

[47] Han F., Bahain J., Deng C., Boëda É., Hou Y., & Wei G. （2017）. The earliest evidence of hominid settlement in China: Combined electron spin resonance and uranium series （ESR/U-series） dating of mammalian fossil teeth from Longgupo cave. Quaternary International, 434, 75-83.

[48] Harmand S., Lewis J. E., Feibel C. S., Lepre C. J., Prat S., & Lenoble A. （2015）. 3.3-million-year-old stone tools from Lomekwi 3, West Turkana, Kenya. Nature, 521 （7552）, 310-315.

[49] Hiscock P., O Connor S., Balme J., & Maloney T. （2016）. World's earliest ground-edge axe production coincides with human colonisation of Australia. Australian Archaeology, 81（1）, 2-11.

[50] Holen S. R., Deméré T. A., Fisher D. C., Fullagar R., Paces J. B., & Jefferson G. T. （2017）. A 130,000-year-old archaeological site in southern California, USA. Nature, 544（7651）, 479-483.

[51] Hussain S. T., & Will M. （2020）. Materiality, agency and evolution of lithic technology: An integrated perspective for palaeolithic archaeology. Journal of Archaeological Method and Theory. https://doi. org/10. 1007/s10816-020-09483-6.

[52] Inizan M., Reduron-Ballinger M., Roche H., & Tixier J. （1995）. Technologie de la pierre taillée. Tome 4. Meudon: CREP.

[53] Inizan M., Reduron-Ballinger M., Roche H., & Tixier J. （1999）. Technology and terminology of knapped stone. Nanterre: CREP.

[54] Jaubert J. （2011）. Préhistoires de France. France: Confluences.

[55] J. -P. Lhomme, & J. -G. Marcillaud. DAPAC/SDAP—Service archéologique départemental des Yvelines （SADY）. https://archeologie. yvelines. fr/.

[56] Kathy D. Schick, & Nicholas Toth. （1993）. Making silent stones speak: Human evolution and the dawn of technology. New York: Simon and Schuster.

[57] Lepot M. （1993）. Approche techno-fonctionnelle de l'outillage lithique Moustérien: essai de classification des parties actives en terme d'efficacité technique. PhD thesis. Paris: University of Paris X.

[58] Li Y., Sun X., & Bodin E. （2014）. A macroscopic technological perspective on lithic production from the Early to Late Pleistocene in the Hanshui River Valley, central

China. Quaternary International, 347, 148-162.

[59]Lourdeau A. (2010). Le technocomplexe Itaparica: définition techno-fonctionnelle des industries à pièces façonnées unifacialement à une face plane dans le centre et le nord-est du Brésil pendant la transition Pléistocène-Holocène et l'Holocène ancien. PhD thesis. Paris: Université Paris Ouest Nanterre La Défense.

[60] Manclossi F. (2016). De la Pierre aux Métaux: dynamiques des changements techniques dans les industries lithiques au Levant Sud, IVe-Ier millénaire av. J. -C. PhD thesis. Paris: Université Paris-Ouest-Nanterre-La-Défense.

[61]Manclossi F., Rosen S. A., & Boëda E. (2019). From stone to metal: the dynamics of technological change in the decline of chipped stone tool production a case study from the Southern Levant (5th-1st Millennia BCE). Journal of Archaeological Method and Theory, 26(4), 1276-1326.

[62]Odell G., Schiffer M. (2003). Lithic analysis. Boston, MA: Springer. Pelegrin J. (1991). Les savoir-faire: une très longue histoire. Terrain, (16), 106-113.

[63]Pérez A., Uceda S., Boëda E., Silva E., Carrión L., & Romero R. (2020). Cobbles, tools, and plants: Techno-functional variability within lithic industries of complex societies in Central Coast, Peru (~1800−400 BP). Journal of Archaeological Science: Reports, 34, 102584. https://doi. org/10. 1016/j. jasrep. 2020. 102584.

[64]Perlès C. (1980). Économie de la matière première et économie du *débitage*: deux exemples grecs. In: J. Tixier (Ed. ), Préhistoire et Technologie lithique (pp. 37-41). Paris: CNRS.

[65]Perlès C. (1991). Économie des matières premières et économie du *débitage*: deux conceptions opposées ? 25 ans d'études technologiques en préhistoire (XIe Rencontres Internationales d'Archéologie et d'Histoire d'Antibes) (pp. 35-45). Juan-les-Pins: Éditions APDCA.

[66]Rocca R. (2013). Peut-on définir des aires culturelles au Paléolithique inférieur ? Originalité des premières industries lithiques en Europe centrale dans le cadre du peuplement de l'Europe. PhD thesis. Paris: Université Paris Nanterre.

[67]Shea J. J. (2020). Prehistoric stone tools of Eastern Africa: A guide. Cambridge: Cambridge University Press.

[68] Shumon H. (2019). The French-Anglophone divide in lithic research. A plea for pluralism in Palaeolithic archaeology. PhD thesis. Netherlands: Leiden University.

[69] Sigaut F. (1991). Un couteau ne sert pas à couper mais en coupant. Structure, fonctionnement et fonction dans l'analyse des objets. 25 ans d'études technologiques en préhistoire：Bilan et perspectives, 21-34.

[70] Simondon G. (1989). Du mode d'existence des objets techniques. Paris：Aubier.

[71] Soriano S. (2000). Outillage bifacial et outillage sur éclat au Paléolithique ancien et moyen：coexistence et interaction. Doctorat thesis. Université de Paris X-Nanterre.

[72] Summerhayes G. R., Leavesley M., Fairbairn A., Mandui H., Field J., & Ford A. (2010). Human adaptation and plant use in highland New Guinea 49,000 to 44,000 years ago. Science, 330(6000), 78-81.

[73] Toro-Moyano I., de Lumley H., Fajardo B., Barsky D., Cauche D., & Celiberti V. (2009). L'industrie lithique des gisements du Pléistocène inférieur de Barranco León et Fuente Nueva3 à Orce, Grenade, Espagne. L'Anthropologie, 113(1), 111-124.

[74] Wei G., Huang W., Chen S., He C., Pang L., & Wu Y. (2014). Paleolithic culture of Longgupo and its creators. Quaternary International, 354(0), 154-161.

[75] Wei G., Huang W., Boëda E., Forestier H., He C., & Chen S. (2017). Recent discovery of a unique Paleolithic industry from the Yumidong Cave site in the Three Gorges region of Yangtze River, southwest China. Quaternary International, 434, Part A, 107-120.

[76] Zhou Y. (2021). Diversity and homogeneity：The lithic technology in southwest China from the late Pleistocene to early Holocene and its implication to Southeast Asia Prehistory. PhD thesis. Paris：ED227, Muséum National d'Histoire Naturelle.

[77] Zhu Z., Dennell R., Huang W., Wu Y., Qiu S., & Yang S. (2018). Hominin occupation of the Chinese Loess Plateau since about 2. 1 million years ago. Nature, 559 (7715), 608-612.

## (2) 中文文献

[1] Boëda E, 侯雪梅. 旧石器时代东亚、西亚之间的关系[J]. 第四纪研究, 2004, 24.

[2] 高星. 制作工具在人类演化中的地位与作用[J]. 人类学学报, 2018, 37(3).

[3] 高星. 中国旧石器时代手斧的特点与意义[J]. 人类学学报, 2012, 31(2).

[4] 高星, 张晓凌, 杨东亚, 等. 现代中国人起源与人类演化的区域性多样化模式[J]. 中国科学：地球科学, 2010(9).

[5] 高星, 侯亚梅. 中国科学院古脊椎动物与古人类研究所 20 世纪旧石器时代考古学研

究[M].北京：文物出版社，2002.

[6]高星，沈辰.石器微痕分析的考古学实验研究[M].北京：科学出版社，2008.

[7]高星，刘武.人类演化的足迹-纪念裴文中先生百年诞辰论文集[J].人类学学报，2004，23(增刊).

[8]高星等.中国古人类石器技术与生存模式的考古学阐释[J].第四纪研究，2006(4).

[9]高星.听，古老的石器在说话[N].光明日报，2022-05-15.

[10]李锋，李英华，高星.贵州观音洞遗址石制品的剥片技术辨析[J].人类学学报，2020(1)

[11]李锋，高星.东亚现代人来源的考古学思考：证据与解释[J].人类学学报，2018，37(2).

[12]李英华.旧石器技术：理论与实践[M].北京：社会科学文献出版社，2017.

[13]李英华，侯亚梅，Bodin E.法国旧石器技术研究概述[J].人类学学报，2008(1).

[14]林圣龙.中西方旧石器文化中的技术模式的比较[J].人类学学报，1996(1).

[15]吕遵谔.中国考古学研究的世纪回顾·旧石器时代考古卷[M].北京：科学出版社，2004.

[16]王幼平.旧石器时代考古[M].北京：文物出版社，2000.

[17]王幼平.石器研究——旧石器时代考古方法初探[M].北京：北京大学出版社，2006.

[18]王幼平.中国远古人类文化的源流[M].北京：科学出版社，2005.

[19]王幼平.更新世环境与中国南方旧石器文化发展[M].北京：北京大学出版社，1997.

[20]吴新智、徐欣.探秘远古人类[M].北京：外语教学与研究出版社，2015.

[21]张森水.中国旧石器文化[M].天津：天津科学技术出版社，1987.

[22]张森水.步迹录：张森水旧石器考古论文集[M].北京：科学出版社，2004.

[23]张森水.近20年来中国旧石器考古学的进展与思考[J].第四纪研究，2002(1).

[24]周玉端，李英华.从遗物展示到技术阐释：法国旧石器绘图方式的变迁和启示[J].考古，2019(2).

[25]周玉端，李英华.旧石器类型学与技术学的回顾与反思[J].考古，2021(2).